Kid-O's Pasta & Turkey Meatballs (page 41)

# INSTANT POT®
## FAMILY MEALS

PHOTOGRAPHY BY
**ERIN SCOTT**

weldon**owen**

# CONTENTS

Turkey Lettuce Wraps
with Hoisin-Peanut
Sauce (page 22)

Veggie Fried Rice with Cashews
(page 114)

# INTRODUCTION

A boon for busy families, the Instant Pot® burst onto the cooking scene in 2009, and there's every indication it has serious staying power. The multifaceted countertop kitchen appliance is loved by hundreds of thousands of families who use it to transform economical cuts of meat into melt-in-your-mouth perfection; create one-pot pasta dishes on busy weeknights; cook nourishing soups; and prepare healthy staples like homemade stocks, cooked beans, and tender whole grains to have on hand for future meals. And the Instant Pot®'s flexible functionality means you can retire your pressure cooker, slow cooker, rice cooker, and yogurt maker—freeing up a lot of countertop real estate, and streamlining your cooking, in the process.

The Instant Pot® can sear, sauté, steam, and pressure cook all in one pot, and in hours less than it would take to cook on the stove top or in the oven, so it's a huge asset for frazzled parents challenged to get dinner on the table. Crowd-pleasing recipes like tender beef tips and whipped potatoes (page 53) cook in just 10 minutes, comforting chicken potpie (page 21) in 10 minutes, and creamy risotto (pages 91 and 115) in just 8 minutes—without constant stirring.

Arguably best in the Instant Pot® are large chunks of meat like pork shoulder and beef chuck roast, which cook up every bit as deliciously as in a slow cooker but hours and hours faster. There are also loads of sleeper hits that utilize the pot's special attributes to cook perfectly—think juicy, Cheddar-stuffed turkey burgers (page 27), spaghetti carbonara (page 75), and broccoli-Cheddar bagel strata (page 109), to name a few.

Soups, such as chicken taco (page 39) and scallop chowder (page 95), become intensely delicious when cooked under pressure. And quicker than your kids can ask "What's for dinner?" the Instant Pot® can cook a complete meal—protein, vegetable, and starch—all at once, using the layering method (aka "pot-in-pot" cooking, see page 17). Did we mention that the Instant Pot® can keep food safely warm, so everyone in the clan can enjoy a healthy, hot meal, no matter when they get home? Yes, the Instant Pot® really is indispensable!

With the following recipes and some knowledge of the appliance's basic functions, Instant Pot®-ing will become your favorite kitchen technique. So let's get cooking!

# COOKING WITH THE INSTANT POT®

The Instant Pot® is available in different models and sizes, with slightly varying attributes, but all accomplish the same basic functions. Once you are accustomed to cooking with it, the specialized functions will become intuitive. As with most new appliances, the best way to master the Instant Pot® is simply to use it.

The recipes in this book were developed with the 6-quart (6-L) Instant Pot® models in mind and use the Sauté and Manual/Pressure Cook functions most often, but the other functions are helpful for a wide range of kitchen tasks. Here's how they work.

**Sauté:** This function allows you to sear meats, simmer liquids, and reduce sauces in the same way you would in a sauté pan on the stove top. It has three modes: Low (Less on some models) is ideal for gently simmering, Medium (Normal on some models) is best for simmering and sautéing, and High (More on some models) can be used for searing and browning. The timer on this function is automatically set for 30 minutes, but in the rare case when you might need it on for longer, just press the Sauté button again after it shuts off and continue cooking. Never put the locking lid on the appliance while using this function.

**Pressure Cook:** There are two levels for pressure cooking—High and Low. Most recipes call for the High setting, but pay attention to when a recipe indicates using the Low setting (usually for more delicate foods like pasta or vegetables). Press the Pressure Level key or Adjust key (depending on your model) to adjust the pressure levels, and the +/- buttons to change the cooking time. (The Lux 6-in-1 V3 model does not have a low-pressure setting.)

**Pressure Release Valve:** Recipes in this book specify either a natural release or quick-release of steam. Natural release means that after the cooking cycle is done, you leave the pressure valve turned to Sealing and the pressure slowly releases on its own. This helps keep beans intact and slowly relaxes meat fibers in roasts, allowing juices to redistribute. It's also used with soup recipes and other dishes containing a lot of liquid, fat, or foam where there will be lots of steam releasing and more potential for hot liquid sputtering out of the valve. Natural release can take anywhere from a few minutes to half an hour, depending on the quantity of food and liquid in the pot.

Quick-release is best for quick-cooking cuts of meat and vegetables. To quick-release the steam, use a long-handled spoon to carefully move the Pressure Release handle on the lid to Venting (or press the valve button down on Ultra models). Be careful, as the steam will be very hot, and steam burns really hurt! Once the steam has stopped and the silver pin in the lid (the float valve) has dropped, unlock and lift the lid away from you to prevent the steam or condensation from injuring you.

In some recipes, both release methods are used by letting the steam release naturally for 10 minutes or so, followed by a quick-release. This is factored into the cooking time, so be sure to follow the instructions accordingly.

Pork Verde & Pinto Bean Tostadas
(page 67)

## THE PRESET BUTTONS

The Instant Pot® includes a range of food-specific buttons, such as Soup/Broth, Meat/Stew, Bean/Chili, Poultry, Cake, and Egg. They correspond to factory-set pressure-cooking times and don't automatically know how to cook certain foods; they are just typical cooking times. You can adjust the times using the +/- buttons and the pot will remember it the next time you choose that button, so it's convenient for recipes you make frequently.

**Slow Cook:** This is a non-pressure-cooking program, where the Low, Medium, and High modes correspond to the keep warm, low, and high settings of most slow cookers. It works similarly to a traditional slow-cooker appliance. You can use this function for preparing your favorite slow-cooker recipes that include a lot of liquid, such as soups and stews.

**Steam:** The Instant Pot®'s steaming function works by warming water under constant, intense heat to cook dense foods like artichokes and potatoes. When using this program, always place the ingredients on the steam rack that came with the pot or on a steaming basket with feet, as food can scorch if it's in direct contact with the bottom of the pot.

**Sterilize:** Some models have a Sterilize function, which is handy for sterilizing baby bottles, baby food jars, and jam jars easily and efficiently. However, the machine is not safe for pressure canning.

**Rice:** This setting cooks white rice under low pressure according to the weight of rice added to the pot. Rinse and drain the rice and use a 1:1 ratio of rice-to-water for best results. Let the steam release naturally for 10 minutes, then quick-release any residual steam.

**Multigrain:** This preset button is designed for long-cooking grains like brown rice and wild rice. Less/Low will cook for 20 minutes, Normal/Medium for 40 minutes, and More/High will warm and soak grains for 45 minutes and then cook them for 60 minutes under high pressure, ideal for very hard grains like hominy.

**Yogurt:** This function features three temperature settings for making homemade yogurt, allowing you to pasteurize and incubate milk at perfect temperatures for fermented dairy products like yogurt, crème fraîche, and fermented glutinous rice.

**Keep Warm/Cancel:** These buttons (combined into one button on some models) turn off any cooking program, allowing you to switch to another program or to end cooking. Keep Warm will keep the food at a safe temperature for up to 10 hours.

**Delay Start:** This feature allows you to delay the start of cooking. It's particularly handy if you want to soak beans before cooking them.

## PRESSURE COOKER PRIMER

Instant Pot® pressure cooking starts with these basic steps:

- The pot needs a sufficient amount of liquid in order to create steam and come up to pressure. Don't reduce the amount of liquid called for in the recipes in this book or the appliance may not come up to pressure.

- Don't fill the pot more than two-thirds full. When cooking primarily ingredients that expand (big batches of beans, rice, or grains, for example), don't fill the pot more than halfway. Overfilling it may cause the steam vent to clog.

- Be sure the sealing ring inside the lid is securely in place. Cover the pot with the lid and lock it in place, then move the Steam release handle (the valve) to Sealing on top of the pot; this will seal the pot so pressure can build up. The valve will feel loose in the lid and this is normal. (For Ultra models, the valve seals automatically, no turning needed.)

- Press the Pressure Cook (Manual on some models) button. The last time entered will appear in the lighted display. You now have 10 seconds to change the time using the +/- buttons and to adjust the pressure level using the Pressure button, which toggles between Low and High.

- After 10 seconds have elapsed, the pot will beep and the lighted display will read "ON" to indicate the cook cycle has started. A small amount of steam will come out of the area

around the silver pin (float valve) in the lid as the pot comes up to pressure. Once the appliance is up to pressure, the LCD display on the panel will switch to show how much time remains in the cook cycle.

- When the cycle has finished, the pot will beep several times and automatically end cooking. Keep in mind that the contents are still under pressure and will continue to cook until all of the pressure is released. This extra cooking time is accounted for in the recipes.

- Release the pressure using the natural-release or quick-release method as specified in the recipe. CAUTION: The steam coming out of the valve will be very hot; use a long spoon handle to move the valve to Venting. You can also throw a clean towel loosely over the vent to disperse steam so it's not shooting straight onto your kitchen wall or cabinets.

## HIGH-ALTITUDE COOKING

If you are cooking at 3,000 feet and are using the pressure-cooking programs on your Instant Pot®, you will need to increase the cook times by 5 percent. For every 1,000 feet above 3,000, increase the cook times by an additional 5 percent, so cook times would increase by 10 percent at 4,000 feet, 15 percent at 5,000 feet, and so on.

The Instant Pot® is well suited for pot-in-pot cooking, a game-changer when you need to cook healthy, balanced meals for your family with minimal fuss and cleanup. With this time-saving technique, you can prepare a main dish and an accompanying side at the same time by layering ingredients in the pot using a tall trivet and a small baking dish or steamer basket (see page 17).

# TIPS FOR INSTANT POT® SUCCESS

### KEEP YOUR POT CLEAN

Just like your stove and pans, your Instant Pot® must be cleaned. After every use, wash the inner pot, detach and wash the condensation cup on the back of the device, the sealing ring, and the lid. Clean the recessed edge of the pot with a rolled-up paper towel dipped in hot soapy water.

### GET THE POT HOT

To sauté and brown, it's best to add the oil to the pot and let it get hot (it will shimmer) before adding ingredients. The LCD screen will eventually display "hot," but the oil is usually ready for sautéing your ingredients before this.

### DON'T OVERCROWD WHEN BROWNING MEAT

The objective of browning is to create a flavorful base for sauces and broths by caramelizing the natural sugars in meat. If you add too much meat to the pot, it will begin to steam instead of brown. In this book, you'll often be instructed to brown just a handful of the meat; this is sufficient to create loads of flavor and skips the tedium of browning every last bit of meat, saving lots of time.

### ADJUST SPICY INGREDIENTS TO SUIT YOUR FAMILY'S TASTE

Every family has a different tolerance for spice, so recipes in this book include a range when calling for ingredients like curry paste or Cajun seasoning. Remember, you can always add more spice after cooking, but you can't remove it once it's in the pot.

### DEGLAZE

The Instant Pot® will display a "burn" notice and interrupt the cooking cycle if the sensors detect ingredients are burning or sticking on the bottom of the pot. To avoid this, make sure to deglaze and scrape up any browned bits from the bottom of the pot after sautéing or browning, and follow the recipe to add the correct amount of stock, water, or other liquid.

### DON'T DROWN THE DISH

In most cases, ½–1 cup (120–240 ml) of liquid is enough to bring the Instant Pot® up to pressure. Keep in mind that lots of ingredients contribute moisture as they cook—a 2-lb (1-kg) chuck roast will add up to 2½ cups (600 ml) of liquid, and broccoli is about 90% water. Follow the rigorously tested recipes in this book and you'll never have to give it another thought.

### STAND BY

The Instant Pot® is great because once the food is in the pot, you can safely leave it unattended. That said, it's wise to hang around until the appliance has fully come up to pressure, especially if you're riffing on a new recipe or are inexperienced with pressure cooking. Once the cook time starts to count down on the screen, you can let the Instant Pot® do its thing and go about your busy day.

### THICKEN AT THE END

Because the Instant Pot® cooks food in a sealed system, sauces won't reduce as they would in stove-top recipes. Adding thickeners like cornstarch or flour at the start of pressure cooking can cause clumping and settling, and you may get the dreaded "burn" notice. It's best to thicken sauces and gravies right before serving. You can also thicken a sauce by simmering it on the Sauté function with the lid off.

## MAKE IT A MEAL: POT-IN-POT COOKING

Several recipes in this book cook both a main dish and an accompanying side by layering the ingredients in the pot using a metal pan set on a tall trivet. In Instant Pot® parlance, this is called pot-in-pot cooking, or PIP for short. The main dish, such as chicken or pork chops, cooks directly in the Instant Pot®, while a side dish that takes about the same amount of time—rice, sweet potatoes, or polenta—cooks in a steamer basket or in a small baking dish or pan set on a tall trivet above the main dish.

These are the two tools that are particularly useful for this technique:

- Oven-safe baking dish 6–7 inches (15–18 cm) in diameter, or a round metal pan 7 inches (18 cm) in diameter, with a 6-cup (1.4-L) capacity, that fits into the inner pot for "pot-in-pot" and layered cooking.

- Metal trivet with tall (2-inch/5-cm) feet for pot-in-pot and layered cooking.

Baking dishes and tall trivets are inexpensive and easy to find online and in kitchenware stores. Just search for "Instant Pot® baking dish" and "Instant Pot® tall trivet" and you'll find lots of options.

## TOOLS OF THE TRADE

The Instant Pot® is an incredible appliance all by itself, but a few additional items are used in the recipes in this book to expand its possibilities.

1½-quart (1.5-L) round oven-safe baking dish for frittatas and more "baked" dishes

Wire-mesh or silicone steaming basket for eggs and vegetables

Sturdy kitchen tongs for browning meat, transferring ingredients from the pot, and safely lifting a baking dish out of the pot

Fat separator to degrease sauces and gravies

Standard blender or immersion blender or for pureeing soups and baby food

Steam rack with handles to raise and lower pans and dishes, as well as for cooking eggs (Note: This rack comes included with many models; if yours does not have handles, you can create a sling by folding a long piece of aluminum foil into thirds so it can rest underneath the steam rack and extend up on either side like handles.)

Digital instant-read thermometer for checking meat doneness

Chicken Adobo Quinoa Burrito Bowls
(page 36)

# POULTRY

You can serve the potpie family-style in a large casserole dish covered with the crust, or parcel out individual potpies in gratin dishes or bowls, as shown.

# Chicken Potpie with Puff Crust

There's no danger of a soggy crust with this easy and flavorful version
of chicken potpie. The hearty filling is cooked in the Instant Pot®
while you bake the flaky puff pastry crust separately.

**SERVES 4–6**

Put the oil in the Instant Pot®, select Sauté, and adjust to More/High heat.
When the oil is hot, add the bacon and cook, turning occasionally, until
crisp, about 5 minutes. Transfer the bacon to a cutting board and leave
the drippings in the pot. Coarsely chop the bacon and set aside.

Add the onion, carrots, celery, thyme, and sage to the pot and cook, stirring
frequently, until the onion is tender, about 4 minutes. Add the wine and
simmer, stirring with a wooden spoon to scrape up any browned bits, until
nearly evaporated, about 1 minute. Press the Cancel button.

Return the bacon to the pot and add the chicken, stock, potatoes,
½ teaspoon salt, and ¼ teaspoon pepper and stir to combine. Lock
the lid in place and turn the valve to Sealing. Press the Pressure Cook
button and set the cook time for 10 minutes at high pressure.

Meanwhile, preheat the oven to 400°F (200°C). On a lightly floured surface,
unfold the puff pastry and roll out into a rectangle large enough to cover a
2-quart (1.9-L) casserole dish. Alternatively, unfold the pastry and cut it into
4–6 strips or rounds to cover individual gratin dishes or soup bowls with
½-inch (12-mm) overhang all around. Place the pastry on a baking sheet and
prick all over with a fork. Bake until puffed and golden, about 15 minutes.

When the cooking time is up, turn the valve to Venting to quick-release
the steam. Carefully remove the lid and use tongs or 2 forks to pull the
chicken apart into bite-size pieces. Add the peas and lemon zest.

In a small bowl, stir together the cornstarch and cold water. Add to
the pot, select Sauté, and adjust to Normal/Medium heat. Cook, stirring
gently, until the sauce is thickened, about 2 minutes. Season to taste with
salt and pepper. Spoon the filling into a casserole dish or individual gratin
dishes, top with the puff pastry, and serve.

1 tablespoon olive oil

2 slices bacon

1 cup (115 g) chopped yellow
onion

2 carrots, peeled and sliced

2 ribs celery, sliced

1 tablespoon chopped fresh
thyme or 1 teaspoon dried
thyme

1 teaspoon dried sage

¼ cup (60 ml) white wine

1½ lb (680 g) boneless,
skinless chicken thighs,
fat trimmed

1½ cups (350 ml) chicken stock
(page 116 or store-bought)

1 red potato, diced

Kosher salt and black pepper

All-purpose flour, for dusting

1 sheet frozen puff pastry,
thawed

1 cup (140 g) frozen peas,
thawed

1½ teaspoons finely grated
lemon zest

3 tablespoons cornstarch

3 tablespoons cold water

# Turkey Lettuce Wraps with Hoisin-Peanut Sauce

Tasty and thrifty, turkey thighs make a wonderful filling for lettuce wraps, served taco-style with a hoisin-peanut sauce for dipping. The recipe works equally well with bone-in chicken thighs; just reduce the cook time to 18 minutes.

**SERVES 4**

To make the turkey, put the oil in the Instant Pot®, select Sauté, and adjust to More/High heat. Season the turkey all over with salt and pepper. When the oil is hot, brown the turkey on both sides, about 4 minutes per side. Transfer to a plate. Press the Cancel button.

Remove the inner pot, pour off the oil, and return the pot to the appliance. Add 2 tablespoons water, the mushrooms, soy sauce, ginger, vinegar, and garlic, stirring with a wooden spoon to scrape up any browned bits. Return the turkey to the pot.

Lock the lid in place and turn the valve to Sealing. Press the Pressure Cook button and set the cook time for 25 minutes at high pressure.

Meanwhile, make the hoisin-peanut sauce: In a small bowl, whisk together the hot water, peanut butter, hoisin sauce, lime juice, and Sriracha; set aside.

Let the steam release naturally for 10 minutes, then turn the valve to Venting to quick-release any residual steam. Carefully remove the lid and transfer the turkey and mushrooms to a cutting board. Cut the turkey and mushroom caps into bite-size pieces, discarding the skin, bones, and mushroom stems. In a medium bowl, stir together the turkey, mushrooms, water chestnuts, carrot, green onions, and ¼ cup (60 ml) of the cooking liquid.

Mound the turkey mixture in the lettuce leaves and serve with the hoisin-peanut sauce for drizzling or dipping.

## FOR THE TURKEY

**2 tablespoons olive oil**

**2 bone-in turkey thighs (about 2 lb/1 kg)**

**Kosher salt and black pepper**

**3 dried shiitake mushrooms**

**¼ cup (60 ml) low-sodium soy sauce**

**2 tablespoons peeled and coarsely chopped fresh ginger**

**2 tablespoons rice vinegar**

**3 cloves garlic, chopped**

## FOR THE SAUCE

**½ cup (120 ml) hot water**

**¼ cup (70 g) peanut butter**

**3 tablespoons hoisin sauce**

**1 tablespoon fresh lime juice**

**1 teaspoon Sriracha**

**½ cup (80 g) chopped water chestnuts**

**1 large carrot, peeled and julienned or shredded**

**3 green onions, chopped**

**1 head Boston lettuce, separated into individual leaves**

In addition to Boston
or butter lettuce, little gem
or romaine leaves make great
healthy bases for savory fillings.

# Chicken Paprika with Buttered Noodles

Tender chicken in a bright red paprika–sour cream sauce served over egg noodles? Sounds good, but the fact that you can throw everything together in one pot and have it on the table in about 35 minutes? A perfect solution for a weeknight dinner.

**SERVES 4**

Put the oil in the Instant Pot®, select Sauté, and adjust to More/High heat. Season the chicken all over with salt and pepper. When the oil is hot, brown half of the chicken on both sides, about 4 minutes per side. Transfer to a plate. (There's no need to brown the rest of the chicken.)

Add the onion and bell pepper to the pot and cook, stirring frequently, until the vegetables are tender, about 4 minutes. Add the garlic and cook until fragrant, about 45 seconds. Add the wine and simmer, stirring with a wooden spoon to scrape up any browned bits, until nearly evaporated, about 1 minute. Press the Cancel button.

Add the stock, tomatoes, sweet paprika, and bay leaf to the pot and stir to combine. Nestle all of the chicken in the stock mixture. Place a trivet with tall (2-inch/5-cm) feet in the pot over the chicken mixture. In a 7-inch (18-cm) round metal pan with a 6-cup (1.4-L) capacity, combine the noodles and water. Cover tightly with aluminum foil and place on the trivet.

Lock the lid in place and turn the valve to Sealing. Press the Pressure Cook button and set the cook time for 5 minutes at high pressure.

Turn the valve to Venting to quick-release the steam. Carefully remove the lid and remove the pan and trivet. Drain the noodles and toss with the butter; set aside.

Put the flour in a medium bowl and whisk in the sour cream until smooth, then gradually whisk in 1 cup (240 ml) of the cooking liquid. Add to the pot, select Sauté, and adjust to Normal/Medium heat. Cook, stirring gently, until the sauce is bubbly and thickened, about 2 minutes. Season to taste with salt and pepper and sprinkle with the smoked paprika. Serve the chicken and sauce over the noodles.

**2 tablespoons olive oil**

**2 lb (1 kg) boneless, skinless chicken thighs, cut in half, fat trimmed**

**Kosher salt and black pepper**

**1 yellow onion, chopped**

**1 red bell pepper, seeded and chopped**

**4 cloves garlic, thinly sliced**

**¼ cup (60 ml) dry white wine or lager beer**

**½ cup (120 ml) chicken stock (page 116 or store-bought)**

**½ cup (125 g) drained diced canned tomatoes**

**4 teaspoons sweet paprika**

**1 bay leaf**

**6 oz (170 g) dried wide egg noodles (about 4 cups)**

**3½ cups (825 ml) water**

**1 tablespoon unsalted butter, at room temperature**

**2 tablespoons all-purpose flour**

**½ cup (115 g) sour cream**

**A few pinches of smoked paprika, for garnish**

# Chicken Scarpariello

Chicken, Italian sausage, and sweet Peppadew peppers combine to make a delicious and adaptable Italian-American dish. Serve with garlic bread to mop up the tangy sauce, toss with rigatoni for a hearty pasta bowl, or ladle over creamy polenta.

### SERVES 4

Put the oil in the Instant Pot®, select Sauté, and adjust to More/High heat. When the oil is hot, add the sausages and cook, stirring occasionally, until browned, about 5 minutes. Transfer to a plate. Add the onion, bell pepper, and garlic to the pot and cook, stirring frequently, until the vegetables are tender, about 4 minutes. Add the wine, stirring with a wooden spoon to scrape up any browned bits. Press the Cancel button.

Add the browned sausage, chicken, Peppadew peppers, vinegar, and rosemary to the pot, season with salt and pepper, and stir to combine.

Lock the lid in place and turn the valve to Sealing. Press the Pressure Cook button and set the cook time for 20 minutes at high pressure.

When the cooking time is up, turn the valve to Venting to quick-release the steam. Carefully remove the lid.

In a small bowl, stir together the cornstarch and water. Add to the pot, select Sauté, and adjust to Normal/Medium heat. Simmer, stirring occasionally, until the sauce is thickened and bubbly, about 2 minutes. Serve the chicken with garlic bread, pasta, or polenta and pass the cheese at the table.

**1 tablespoon olive oil**

**1 lb (450 g) turkey or chicken Italian sausages, casings removed, sausages broken into bite-size pieces**

**1 yellow onion, sliced through root end**

**1 large red bell pepper, seeded and sliced**

**4 cloves garlic, minced**

**¼ cup (60 ml) dry white wine**

**2 lb (1 kg) bone-in chicken thighs, skin removed, excess fat trimmed**

**¼ cup (45 g) Peppadew peppers or other sweet pickled peppers, coarsely chopped**

**2 tablespoons red wine vinegar or balsamic vinegar**

**2 fresh rosemary sprigs**

**Kosher salt and black pepper**

**2 teaspoons cornstarch**

**2 teaspoons cold water**

**Garlic bread, pasta, or polenta, for serving**

**1 cup (115 g) grated Parmesan cheese, for serving**

# Juicy Turkey Burgers

Steaming burgers in the Instant Pot® turns out juicy patties without all the greasy mess that panfrying produces. This turkey version is stuffed with Cheddar cheese for an extra-yummy burger with a surprise hidden inside. Complete the meal with waffle fries and a green salad.

**SERVES 6**

In a large bowl, combine the turkey, mayonnaise, mustard, and seasoning salt and mix gently with your hands until well blended. Divide the meat into 6 even-size balls. Place one portion of the meat mixture in the palm of your hand and place a piece of cheese in the center. Form into a 4-inch (10-cm) patty, making sure the cheese is enclosed in the center of the meat. Wrap in aluminum foil. Repeat with the remaining meat and cheese to make a total of 6 foil-wrapped patties.

Pour ½ cup (120 ml) water into the Instant Pot®. Place a trivet with handles in the pot. Place the foil-wrapped patties on the trivet, layering them as needed.

Lock the lid in place and turn the valve to Sealing. Press the Pressure Cook button and set the cook time for 15 minutes at high pressure.

Turn the valve to Venting to quick-release the steam. Carefully remove the lid and transfer the burgers to a plate.

Carefully unwrap the burgers. Place them on the buns, top with the lettuce and pickles, and serve the ketchup on the side.

2 lb (1 kg) ground turkey (a mix of dark and white meat)

¼ cup (60 ml) plus 2 tablespoons mayonnaise

2 teaspoons Dijon or yellow mustard

¾ teaspoon seasoning salt

Six ¼-inch-thick (6.3-mm) pieces Cheddar cheese, each about 2 inches (5 cm) long by 1 inch (2.5 cm) wide

6 hamburger buns, toasted

6 lettuce leaves

Hamburger pickle slices, for serving

Ketchup, for serving

# Chicken Drumsticks with Thai Peanut Sauce

If your family loves salad rolls with peanut sauce, they'll love this chicken dish with creamy peanut sauce. Leave the skin on the drumsticks; the Instant Pot® makes the meat so succulent that it will fall off the bone if the skin is removed before cooking. Adjust the amount of Thai curry paste according to your family's taste for spice. Serve with steamed broccoli and jasmine rice (see Tip).

**SERVES 4**

In the Instant Pot®, whisk together the onion, garlic, lemongrass, soy sauce, vinegar, brown sugar, and curry paste. Add the chicken drumsticks and stir to coat.

Lock the lid in place and turn the valve to Sealing. Press the Pressure Cook button and set the cook time for 20 minutes at high pressure.

When the cooking time is up, turn the valve to Venting to quick-release the steam. Carefully remove the lid, transfer the drumsticks to a serving platter, and tent with aluminum foil. Remove the lemongrass and discard.

Whisk the coconut cream and peanut butter into the cooking liquid until smooth. Do not heat the sauce or it will thicken too much. Pour the sauce over the chicken and serve right away.

**TIP** *Note that 1 teaspoon of Thai curry paste will make a very mild sauce, while 1 tablespoon will yield a fairly spicy one. If using boneless, skinless chicken thighs, reduce the cook time to 5 minutes. You can cook rice at the same time by combining 1½ cups (300 g) jasmine rice and 1½ cups (350 ml) water in a baking dish or round metal pan; cover tightly with foil and place on a tall trivet set in the pot over the chicken.*

**1 yellow onion, chopped**

**6 cloves garlic, chopped**

**1 lemongrass stalk, halved lengthwise**

**¼ cup (60 ml) low-sodium soy sauce**

**¼ cup (60 ml) rice vinegar**

**2 tablespoons light brown sugar**

**1 teaspoon–1 tablespoon Thai red curry paste**

**8 skin-on chicken drumsticks**

**½ cup (120 ml) unsweetened coconut cream**

**½ cup (140 g) peanut butter**

# Marinated Indian Chicken

Chicken breasts are a blank canvas for absorbing the curry flavors in this marinade, while the yogurt makes the meat incredibly tender and juicy. Be sure to use thick jarred Indian curry paste, not thinner simmer sauces. Look for the paste where Indian ingredients are sold in the grocery store and online. Serve with basmati rice or packaged garlic naan.

### SERVES 4

In a nonaluminum container or bowl, whisk together the yogurt, curry paste, turmeric, and ¼ teaspoon each salt and pepper. Add the chicken and toss to coat. Cover and refrigerate for at least 1 hour and up to 24 hours.

Put the oil in the Instant Pot®, select Sauté, and adjust to Normal/Medium heat. When the oil is hot, add the onion and cook, stirring frequently, until beginning to brown, about 5 minutes. Add the garlic and ginger and cook until fragrant, about 30 seconds. Press the Cancel button. Add the chicken and marinade and the stock, and stir to combine.

Lock the lid in place and turn the valve to Sealing. Press the Pressure Cook button and set the cook time for 4 minutes at high pressure.

Let the steam release naturally for 10 minutes, then turn the valve to Venting to quick-release any remaining steam. Carefully remove the lid and serve the chicken with a few tablespoons of the cooking liquid spooned over the top.

**TIP** *If using boneless chicken thighs, increase the cook time to 10 minutes. Whole bone-in chicken (skin removed) can also be used. For bone-in chicken thighs, increase the cook time to 15 minutes. Cook bone-in chicken breasts for 7 minutes.*

½ **cup (130 g) plain yogurt**

**3 tablespoons Indian curry paste (such as Patak's)**

**1 teaspoon ground turmeric**

**Kosher salt and black pepper**

**1½ lb (680 g) boneless, skinless chicken breasts, cut into 1½-inch (4-cm) pieces**

**1 tablespoon canola oil or ghee**

**1 yellow onion, thinly sliced through root end**

**3 cloves garlic, chopped**

**1 tablespoon minced peeled fresh ginger**

½ **cup (120 ml) chicken stock (page 116 or store-bought)**

# Chicken Thighs with Garlic Gravy & Celery Root Mashed Potatoes

Whole garlic cloves become mild and creamy when cooked in the Instant Pot®, almost as if they've been roasted. They make a perfect sauce for tasty chicken thighs. Celery root is a knobby root vegetable that tastes mildly of celery;

**SERVES 4–6**

Put the oil in the Instant Pot®, select Sauté, and adjust to More/High heat. Season the chicken all over with salt and pepper. When the oil is hot, working in batches, brown the chicken until golden brown on one side, about 4 minutes. Transfer to a plate.

Add the shallot and garlic to the pot and cook, stirring occasionally, until the shallot begins to brown, about 3 minutes. Add the wine, stirring with a wooden spoon to scrape up any browned bits. Press the Cancel button.

Add the stock to the pot and stir to combine. Return the chicken and any accumulated juices to the pot. Place a steamer basket over the chicken and put the celery root and potato in it.

Lock the lid in place and turn the valve to Sealing. Press the Pressure Cook button and set the cook time for 20 minutes at high pressure.

When the cooking time is up, turn the valve to Venting to quick-release the steam. Carefully remove the lid. Using a large spoon, transfer the celery root and potato to a large bowl. Add 2½ tablespoons of the butter and mash until smooth. Stir in the cream and nutmeg. Season to taste with salt and pepper and cover to keep warm. Remove the steamer basket from the pot.

**2 tablespoons canola oil**

**8 bone-in chicken thighs, skin removed, excess fat trimmed**

**Kosher salt and black pepper**

**1 cup (100 g) sliced shallot**

**10 cloves garlic, peeled and left whole**

**¼ cup (60 ml) dry white wine**

**¼ cup (60 ml) chicken stock (page 116 or store-bought)**

**1 large celery root (about 1½ lb/680 g), peeled and cut into 1-inch (2.5-cm) pieces**

**1 large russet potato (about 15 oz/425 g), peeled and cut into 1½-inch (4-cm) pieces**

here it cooks with potatoes to create a silky mash with a healthy dose of B vitamins and fiber. For an added boost of veggies, you can also serve this flavorful dish with a side of steamed vegetables (page 118).

Transfer the chicken to a serving platter and tent with aluminum foil. Select Sauté and adjust to Normal/Medium heat. Using a ladle, skim off the fat from the cooking liquid.

In a small bowl, stir together the remaining 1½ tablespoons butter and the flour until smooth. Whisk into the pot in 2 additions. Bring to a simmer and cook, stirring occasionally, until thickened and bubbly, about 2 minutes. Season the gravy to taste with salt and pepper, spoon over the chicken, and serve with the celery root mashed potatoes, sprinkled with the parsley.

**TIP** *Softened butter mixed with flour, called beurre manié in French, works just like the flour-fat roux that's used at the beginning of cooking to thicken gravy and white sauce. The only difference is that beurre manié is added at the end of cooking. It makes sauces deliciously silky and works brilliantly for Instant Pot® cooking.*

**4 tablespoons (½ stick/ 60 g) unsalted butter, at room temperature**

**¼ cup (60 ml) heavy cream, warmed**

**½ teaspoon ground nutmeg**

**1½ tablespoons all-purpose flour**

**¼ cup (15 g) minced fresh flat-leaf parsley**

# Honey Barbecue Wings with Homemade Ranch Dip

These sweet and tangy wings are a breeze to make and can be cooked in the Instant Pot® ahead, then finished under the broiler when you're ready to party. Serve with carrot and celery sticks.

## SERVES 4

To make the wings, in a large bowl, toss the chicken wings with the chili powder, ½ teaspoon salt, and ¼ teaspoon pepper. Pour 1 cup (240 ml) water into the Instant Pot® and place a steamer basket in the pot. Arrange the wings in the basket.

Lock the lid in place and turn the valve to Sealing. Press the Pressure Cook button and set the cook time for 5 minutes at high pressure.

When the cooking time is up, turn the valve to Venting to quick-release the steam. Carefully remove the lid.

Place a rack so it is 4 inches (10 cm) below the broiler element and preheat the broiler. Line a baking sheet with aluminum foil and spray with nonstick cooking spray.

To make the barbecue sauce, in a medium bowl, stir together the ketchup, honey, mustard, oil, Worcestershire sauce, lemon juice, and garlic powder.

Using tongs, carefully dip each wing piece in the barbecue sauce and place on the prepared baking sheet. Broil the wings until browned and crispy on the edges, about 5 minutes. Flip with tongs and cook on the other side until browned, 5 minutes longer.

Meanwhile, make the ranch dip: In a medium bowl, whisk together the yogurt, mayonnaise, buttermilk, chives, dill, garlic powder, and pepper.

Transfer the wings to a platter and serve the dip on the side.

### FOR THE WINGS AND BARBECUE SAUCE

**3 lb (1.4 kg) "party" chicken wings (separated at the joints)**

**2 teaspoons mild or medium chili powder**

**Kosher salt and black pepper**

**½ cup (115 g) ketchup**

**¼ cup (90 g) honey**

**1½ tablespoons Dijon mustard**

**1 tablespoon toasted sesame oil**

**1½ teaspoons Worcestershire sauce**

**1½ teaspoons fresh lemon juice**

**½ teaspoon garlic powder**

### FOR THE RANCH DIP

**½ cup (115 g) plain Greek yogurt**

**½ cup (120 ml) mayonnaise**

**¼ cup (60 ml) buttermilk**

**2 tablespoons minced fresh chives or green onions**

**2 tablespoons chopped fresh dill or 1 teaspoon dried dill**

**¼ teaspoon garlic powder**

**⅛ teaspoon black pepper**

If you'd prefer to skip the mayonnaise in the ranch dip, double the amount of yogurt or—for a cheesy variation—swap the mayonnaise for ¼ cup (35 g) crumbled blue cheese and omit the dill.

# Honey Chicken Cashew Un-Stir-Fry with Rice

This healthy Chinese takeout–style meal cooks sweet-and-tangy chicken and rice at the same time using the pot-in-pot method (see page 17). The veggies are added after the chicken and rice are done so you get perfectly cooked everything. The recipe is easily adaptable: swap in green beans or snow peas for the broccoli.

**SERVES 4**

Put the canola and sesame oils in the Instant Pot®, select Sauté, and adjust to Normal/Medium heat. When the oil is hot, add the chicken, ½ teaspoon salt, and ¼ teaspoon pepper and cook without stirring until the chicken is opaque white, about 2 minutes. Add the onion and garlic and cook, stirring frequently, until fragrant, about 45 seconds. Press the Cancel button.

In a small bowl, stir together the soy sauce, honey, vinegar, and Sriracha. Add to the pot and stir to combine. Place a trivet with tall (2-inch/5-cm) feet in the pot over the chicken mixture. In a 7-inch (18-cm) round metal pan with a 6-cup (1.4-L) capacity, stir together the rice and 1½ cups (350 ml) water. Cover tightly with aluminum foil and place on the trivet.

Lock the lid in place and turn the valve to Sealing. Press the Pressure Cook button and set the cook time for 5 minutes at high pressure.

When the cooking time is up, turn the valve to Venting to quick-release the steam. Carefully remove the lid and remove the pan and trivet. Keep the pan covered with foil.

Add the broccoli and bell pepper to the pot, select Sauté, and adjust to More/High heat. Place a regular pan lid on the pot, bring to a simmer, and cook until the vegetables are crisp-tender, about 3 minutes.

In a small bowl, stir together the cornstarch and the cold water. Add to the pot and cook until the sauce has thickened, about 1 minute. Serve the chicken, vegetables, and rice sprinkled with the cashews.

1 tablespoon canola oil

1 tablespoon toasted sesame oil

1½ lb (680 g) boneless, skinless chicken breasts, cut into 1-inch (2.5-cm) pieces

Kosher salt and black pepper

1 cup (115 g) chopped yellow onion

3 cloves garlic, minced

3 tablespoons low-sodium soy sauce

2 tablespoons honey

2 tablespoons rice vinegar

1 teaspoon–1 tablespoon Sriracha

1½ cups (300 g) long-grain or short-grain (sushi) rice, rinsed and drained

3 cups (170 g) bite-size broccoli florets

1 red bell pepper, seeded and thinly sliced

2 tablespoons cornstarch

2 tablespoons cold water

1 cup (115 g) roasted cashews

# Turkey & Wild Rice Soup

This creamy, nourishing soup is a great way to enjoy leftover roast turkey, or you can use a few thick slabs of smoked turkey from the deli counter of the grocery store, if you like. Earthy wild rice normally takes at least 45 minutes to cook on the stove top, but in the Instant Pot®, it's ready in just 25 minutes.

## SERVES 6

Put the oil in the Instant Pot®, select Sauté, and adjust to More/High heat. When the oil is hot, add the onion, carrots, celery, mushrooms, thyme, sage, and a pinch of salt and cook, stirring occasionally, until the onion is tender and the mushrooms have given off their liquid, about 6 minutes. Add the sherry and simmer, stirring with a wooden spoon to scrape up any browned bits, until nearly evaporated, about 2 minutes. Press the Cancel button. Add the stock, wild rice, and bay leaves.

Lock the lid in place and turn the valve to Sealing. Press the Pressure Cook button and set the cook time for 25 minutes at high pressure.

Let the steam release naturally for 15 minutes, then turn the valve to Venting to quick-release any residual steam. Carefully remove the lid and remove the bay leaves and discard. Add the turkey and cream and stir to combine. Select Sauté, adjust to Normal/Medium heat, and simmer until heated through, about 5 minutes. Season to taste with salt and pepper.

Ladle the soup into bowls and serve.

**TIP** *Don't miss the deliciousness of homemade turkey stock! The Instant Pot® extracts 100% of the flavor and goodness from the leftover bones of a roast turkey. Just combine the bones with 8 cups (1.9 L) water, 1 roughly chopped onion, 2 roughly chopped carrots, 2 sliced ribs celery, and 2 bay leaves and cook for 1 hour at high pressure. Let the pressure release naturally and then strain the stock.*

**2 tablespoons olive oil**

**1 yellow onion, chopped**

**2 carrots, peeled and chopped**

**3 ribs celery, sliced**

**½ lb (225 g) cremini mushrooms, brushed clean and sliced**

**2 teaspoons chopped fresh thyme or ¾ teaspoon dried thyme**

**½ teaspoon dried sage**

**Kosher salt and black pepper**

**½ cup (120 ml) dry sherry or white wine**

**6 cups (1.4 L) chicken stock (page 116 or store-bought) or turkey stock (see Tip)**

**1 cup (155 g) wild rice**

**2 bay leaves**

**1 lb (450 g) roast turkey or smoked turkey breast, cut into bite-size pieces**

**¼ cup (60 ml) heavy cream**

# Chicken Adobo Quinoa Burrito Bowls

Flavorful Filipino-style chicken pairs beautifully with nutty quinoa, buttery corn, and earthy black beans for a tasty bowl. Everything is cooked in the Instant Pot® at the same time, so it makes a great weeknight dinner. Serve in bowls, or wrap up the ingredients in burrito-size flour tortillas with grated jack cheese for a handheld, do-ahead meal.

**SERVES 4**

In the Instant Pot®, whisk together the vinegar, soy sauce, brown sugar, ginger, and garlic. Add the chicken and onion and stir to coat with the sauce.

Place a trivet with tall (2-inch/5-cm) feet in the pot over the chicken mixture. In a 7-inch (18-cm) round metal pan with a 6-cup (1.4-L) capacity, stir together the quinoa and water. Place the beans and corn on top but don't stir. Cover tightly with aluminum foil and place on the trivet.

Lock the lid in place and turn the valve to Sealing. Press the Pressure Cook button and set the cook time for 12 minutes at high pressure.

When the cooking time is up, turn the valve to Venting to quick-release the steam. Carefully remove the lid and remove the pan and trivet.

Divide the quinoa, beans, and corn among 4 bowls. Top with the chicken, discarding the cooking liquid. Garnish with the pico de gallo and avocado and serve.

¼ cup (60 ml) apple cider vinegar

2 tablespoons low-sodium soy sauce

1½ teaspoons firmly packed light brown sugar

1 tablespoon peeled and sliced fresh ginger

3 cloves garlic, chopped

1 lb (450 g) boneless, skinless chicken thighs

1 yellow onion, thinly sliced through root end

¾ cup (130 g) quinoa, rinsed and drained

¾ cup (180 ml) plus 1 tablespoon water

1 cup (170 g) canned black beans, rinsed and drained

½ cup (90 g) frozen corn, thawed

1 cup (240 ml) pico de gallo

1 avocado, pitted, peeled, and diced

These nourishing, hearty bowls are easy to customize. Family members can choose their preferred toppings; try shredded Cheddar cheese, chopped fresh herbs, or diced steamed vegetables.

# Chicken Zoodle Soup

Spiralized-cut zucchini strands, aka "zoodles," replace regular egg noodles in this lighter spin on the classic soup. Have the kids help spiralize—it's great fun! Lemon and fresh dill give the dish a springlike touch. Add fresh shelled peas or asparagus tips with the zoodles, if you like.

**SERVES 6**

Put the oil in the Instant Pot®, select Sauté, and adjust to More/High heat. When the oil is hot, add the onions and celery and cook, stirring frequently, until the vegetables are tender, about 4 minutes. Add the garlic and cook until fragrant, about 30 seconds. Press the Cancel button. Add the stock, chicken, and bay leaf.

Lock the lid in place and turn the valve to Sealing. Press the Pressure Cook button and set the cook time for 8 minutes at high pressure.

When the cooking time is up, turn the valve to Venting to quick-release the steam. Carefully remove the lid and remove the bay leaf and discard. Transfer the chicken to a cutting board and cut into bite-size pieces. Return the chicken to the pot and add the zucchini noodles, dill, and lemon juice. Cover with the lid and let stand with the Instant Pot® off until the zoodles are heated through, about 3 minutes.

Season to taste with salt and pepper. Ladle the soup into bowls and serve.

**1 tablespoon olive oil**

**2 yellow onions, chopped**

**3 ribs celery, sliced**

**2 cloves garlic, chopped**

**6 cups (1.4 L) chicken stock (page 116 or store-bought)**

**2 boneless, skinless chicken breasts (about ½ lb/225 g each)**

**1 bay leaf**

**2 zucchini, spiralized, or 1 package (10 oz/285 g) zucchini noodles**

**2 tablespoons chopped fresh dill**

**1 tablespoon fresh lemon juice**

**Kosher salt and black pepper**

# Chicken Taco Soup

The smoky, fruity flavor of New Mexican chile broth in this cozy soup is accented by an array of creamy, crunchy, and spicy toppings. Invite everyone in your family to garnish their own soup for fun DIY bowls. Look for whole dried New Mexican chiles in packets where Latin foods are sold.

**SERVES 4**

To make the soup, put the chiles in a small bowl, add boiling water to cover, and let soak until softened, about 10 minutes, then drain. Coarsely chop the onion. In a blender or food processor, combine the chiles, onion, tomatoes, garlic, cumin, oregano, 1 teaspoon salt, and ½ teaspoon pepper and blend until smooth, stopping to scrape down the sides. Pour the chile mixture into the Instant Pot®. Swish out the blender or food processor bowl with 1 cup (240 ml) of the stock and pour it into the pot. Add the remaining 3 cups (700 ml) stock, the chicken, and bay leaf and stir to combine.

Lock the lid in place and turn the valve to Sealing. Press the Pressure Cook button and set the cook time for 8 minutes at high pressure.

When the cooking time is up, turn the valve to Venting to quick-release the steam. Carefully remove the lid and remove the bay leaf and discard. Transfer the chicken to a cutting board and cut into bite-size pieces; set aside.

Put the masa in a medium bowl and whisk in 1 cup (240 ml) of the soup. Whisk into the pot, select Sauté, and adjust to Normal/Medium heat. Simmer, stirring occasionally, until thickened, about 2 minutes. Stir in the chicken and season to taste with salt and pepper.

Ladle the soup into bowls. Top with the avocado, cheese, tortilla chips, and sour cream and serve.

**TIP** *Masa harina adds a buttery, corny flavor to this soup and also thickens it. Look for it in the baking aisle or where Latin ingredients are sold. The package will say "for making tortillas."*

### FOR THE SOUP

**2 dried New Mexican chiles, stemmed, seeded, and chopped**

**1 yellow onion**

**1½ cups (375 g) canned crushed tomatoes**

**3 cloves garlic, peeled and left whole**

**2 teaspoons ground cumin**

**1½ teaspoons dried Mexican oregano**

**Kosher salt and black pepper**

**4 cups (940 ml) chicken stock (page 116 or store-bought)**

**1 lb (450 g) boneless, skinless chicken breasts**

**1 bay leaf**

**2 tablespoons corn masa mix (masa harina)**

### FOR SERVING

**1 cup (115 g) grated pepper jack or Cheddar cheese**

**1 avocado, pitted, peeled, and diced**

**2 cups (170 g) coarsely crushed lime-flavored tortilla chips**

**½ cup (115 g) sour cream**

This kid-friendly comfort food gets a double dose of nutty Parmesan, which is used in the meatballs and also in the sauce.

# Kid-O's Pasta & Turkey Meatballs

This homemade pasta-and-meatball recipe tastes reminiscent of the old-school canned version of your childhood, with a slightly sweet tomato sauce, tender mini pasta shapes, and little turkey meatballs. Your kids will love it, and the kid in you will, too.

**SERVES 4**

In a bowl, combine the crushed crackers, milk, and egg yolk and mash with a fork until the crackers are moistened. Add the turkey, 3 tablespoons of the Parmesan, the Italian seasoning, garlic powder, and ¼ teaspoon salt. Using your hands or a wooden spoon, stir gently to combine. Form into 26–30 meatballs, using a heaping teaspoon for each one. Refrigerate for 10 minutes.

In the Instant Pot®, whisk together the stock, tomato sauce, sugar, and ½ teaspoon salt. Add the pasta and stir to combine. Place the meatballs on top but don't stir.

Lock the lid in place and turn the valve to Sealing. Press the Pressure Cook button and set the cook time for 5 minutes at low pressure.

Let the steam release naturally for 5 minutes, then turn the valve to Venting to quick-release any residual steam. Carefully remove the lid. Using a rubber spatula, gently stir in the butter and the remaining ¼ cup Parmesan. Serve right away.

**9 round buttery crackers, finely crushed (1 oz/30 g)**

**1½ tablespoons plain yogurt**

**1 large egg yolk**

**¾ lb (340 g) ground turkey (a mix of dark and white meat is best), or 90% lean ground beef**

**7 tablespoons (50 g) grated Parmesan cheese**

**½ teaspoon dried Italian seasoning**

**¼ teaspoon garlic powder**

**Kosher salt**

**1¼ cups (300 ml) chicken stock (page 116 or store-bought)**

**1 can (15 oz/425 g) tomato sauce**

**1 tablespoon sugar**

**6 oz (170 g) mini dried pasta, such as anelli, farfalle, ditalini, or penne (about 2 cups)**

**3 tablespoons unsalted butter, at room temperature**

Two-Bean No-Soak Beef Chili (page 59)

# BEEF

# Cherry Cola Short Ribs

These fall-apart ribs, which cook alongside plenty of tender carrots, have a crowd-pleasing sauce that's not overtly cherry cola flavored, just a nice balance of sweet and tart thanks to cola + balsamic vinegar. Serve with mashed potatoes, whipped cauliflower, or polenta to catch all of the lovely sauce.

**SERVES 4–6**

Put the oil in the Instant Pot®, select Sauté, and adjust to More/High heat. Season the short ribs all over with salt and pepper. When the oil is hot, working in batches, brown the ribs, meaty side down, about 6 minutes per batch. Transfer to a plate. Remove the inner pot, pour off all but 1 tablespoon of the oil, and return the pot to the appliance.

Add the onion to the pot and cook, stirring frequently, until tender, about 4 minutes. Add the tomato paste and cook until fragrant, about 30 seconds. Press the Cancel button. Add the cherry cola and vinegar, stirring with a wooden spoon to scrape up any browned bits. Return the short ribs to the pot and add the bay leaf. Place the carrots on top but don't stir.

Lock the lid in place and turn the valve to Sealing. Press the Pressure Cook button and set the cook time for 40 minutes at high pressure.

When the cooking time is up, let the steam release naturally for 15 minutes, then turn the valve to Venting to quick-release any residual steam. Carefully remove the lid and remove the bay leaf and discard. Transfer the ribs and carrots to a serving platter. They'll be very tender, so handle them gently or they'll fall apart. Tent with aluminum foil.

Pour the cooking liquid into a fat separator and pour off the fat. Alternatively, pour the cooking liquid into a large glass measuring cup, spoon off the fat, and discard. (There will be as much as ½ cup–2 cups/120–475 ml fat.)

Return the defatted cooking liquid to the pot, select Sauté, and adjust to More/High heat. Simmer until the liquid is reduced by half, about 8 minutes. Pour the sauce over the ribs and carrots and serve.

**2 tablespoons olive oil**

**4 lb (1.8 kg) bone-in beef short ribs**

**Kosher salt and black pepper**

**1 yellow onion, chopped**

**3 tablespoons tomato paste**

**1¼ cups (300 ml) cherry cola**

**1 tablespoon balsamic vinegar**

**1 bay leaf**

**4 large carrots, peeled and cut into large chunks**

# Two-Layer Beef & Guacamole Tacos

These tacos will please both the crispy taco lovers and the soft tortilla fans in your house. Simply slather homemade guacamole on a flour tortilla and wrap it around a corn taco shell filled with melt-in-your-mouth beer-braised beef. Creamy, crunchy, juicy, yummy, all in one bite!

## SERVES 4-6

Put the oil in the Instant Pot®, select Sauté, and adjust to More/High heat. Season the beef all over with salt and pepper. When the oil is hot, add half of the beef and cook until well browned on two sides, about 4 minutes per side. Transfer to a plate. (There's no need to brown the rest of the beef.)

Add the onion to the pot and cook, stirring frequently, until tender, about 4 minutes. Add two-thirds of the garlic and all of the cumin and cook until fragrant, about 30 seconds. Press the Cancel button. Add the salsa and beer, stirring with a wooden spoon to scrape up any browned bits. Add all of the beef and any accumulated juices and the bay leaf.

Lock the lid in place and turn the valve to Sealing. Press the Pressure Cook button and set the cook time for 35 minutes at high pressure.

When the cooking time is up, let the steam release naturally for 25 minutes, then turn the valve to Venting to quick-release any residual steam. Carefully remove the lid and remove the bay leaf and discard. Transfer the beef to a cutting board and cut into bite-size pieces, discarding any fat. Place the beef in a bowl. Using a slotted spoon, transfer the solids from the cooking liquid and scatter them over the beef. Cover to keep warm. Discard the cooking liquid or reserve for another use, like making chili.

In a bowl, mash together the avocado, tomato, and the remaining garlic, and season with salt and pepper. Spread the guacamole evenly on the tortillas. Place a taco shell on top of each tortilla and bring up the sides of the tortilla to adhere them to the shells. Fill the shells with the beef mixture, lettuce, and cheese. Serve with hot sauce on the side.

1 tablespoon olive oil

2 lb (1 kg) boneless beef chuck roast, excess fat trimmed, cut into 6 large pieces

Kosher salt and black pepper

1 yellow onion, chopped

3 cloves garlic, chopped

1 tablespoon ground cumin

1 can (7 oz/198 g) mild salsa

⅓ cup (80 ml) lager beer

1 bay leaf

1 large ripe avocado, pitted and peeled

1 plum tomato, chopped

8 small (6-inch/15-cm) soft flour tortillas

8 crunchy corn taco shells

2 cups (170 g) shredded romaine lettuce

1 cup (115 g) grated Cheddar or jack cheese

Hot sauce, for serving

If you'd like, skip the tortillas and taco shells and serve the flavorful meat and toppings over a bed of chopped romaine lettuce as a salad.

# Ginger Beef & Broccoli

What's the trick to achieving a dish with fall-apart tender beef and al dente broccoli in the Instant Pot®? Microwave-steam the broccoli while the beef braises under pressure in a rich gingery sauce. Then marry the two just before serving. Pair with hot steamed rice for a meal that will rival any takeout dinner.

### SERVES 6

In a large bowl, toss together the beef, rice wine, and white pepper. Let stand for 5 minutes.

Put the safflower oil in the Instant Pot®, select Sauté, and adjust to More/High heat. When the oil is hot, add one small handful of the beef and cook, stirring frequently, until browned, about 1 minute. Add the ginger and garlic and cook until fragrant, 30 seconds. Press the Cancel button. Add the remaining beef, the stock, soy sauce, and oyster sauce to the pot and stir to combine.

Lock the lid in place and turn the valve to Sealing. Press the Pressure Cook button and set the cook time for 12 minutes at high pressure.

Meanwhile, in a microwave-safe bowl, combine the broccoli and 2 tablespoons water. Cover and microwave on High until crisp-tender, about 3 minutes. Drain and set aside, uncovered.

When the cooking time is up, let the steam release naturally for 10 minutes, then turn the valve to Venting to quick-release any residual steam. Carefully remove the lid.

In a small bowl, stir together the cornstarch and the cold water. Add to the pot, select Sauté, and adjust to Normal/Medium heat. Simmer, stirring occasionally, until the liquid is thickened and bubbly, about 4 minutes. Stir in the broccoli and sesame oil and cook until heated through, about 1 minute. Sprinkle with the green onions and serve.

**TIP** *Rice wine adds authentic flavor to stir-fries and marinades. It keeps indefinitely in the pantry.*

2 lb (1 kg) boneless beef chuck roast, excess fat trimmed, meat cut into strips ¼ inch (6 mm) thick

2 tablespoons rice wine or dry sherry (see Tip)

½ teaspoon white pepper

1 tablespoon safflower or canola oil

2 tablespoons peeled and minced fresh ginger

4 cloves garlic, thinly sliced

¾ cup (180 ml) chicken stock (page 116 or store-bought)

¼ cup (60 ml) low-sodium soy sauce

3 tablespoons oyster sauce

¾ lb (340 g) broccoli crowns, cut into florets

2 tablespoons cornstarch

2 tablespoons cold water

1 teaspoon toasted sesame oil

3 green onions, thinly sliced

# Massaman Curry

This mild southern Thai curry calls for massaman curry paste, available online and where Asian ingredients are sold. The dish is usually made with potatoes, but starchy kabocha squash has a similar texture, is tastier, and is nutrient-packed. Serve as a stew or ladle over steamed jasmine rice.

### SERVES 4–6

Cut the squash into enough 1½-inch (4-cm) pieces to measure 3½ cups (455 g). Save the remaining squash for another use; it freezes well.

Put 1 tablespoon of the oil in the Instant Pot®, select Sauté, and adjust to More/High heat. Season the beef all over with salt and pepper. When the oil is hot, add one small handful of the beef and cook, stirring frequently, until well browned, about 4 minutes. Transfer to a plate. (There's no need to brown the rest of the beef.) Add the remaining 1 tablespoon oil and the onion to the pot and cook, stirring frequently, until beginning to brown, about 4 minutes. Add the curry paste and cook until fragrant, about 10 seconds. Press the Cancel button.

Scoop the thick opaque cream off the top of the coconut milk and set aside. Pour the thin coconut milk into the pot, stirring with a wooden spoon to scrape up any browned bits. Add all of the beef, the tamarind paste, and lime leaves. Put the squash on top but don't stir.

Lock the lid in place and turn the valve to Sealing. Press the Pressure Cook button and set the cook time for 25 minutes at high pressure.

When the cooking time is up, let the steam release naturally for 10 minutes, then turn the valve to Venting to quick-release any residual steam. Carefully remove the lid.

In a small bowl, stir together the cornstarch and cold water. Gently stir into the pot, select Sauté, and adjust to Normal/Medium heat. Cook until the curry is thickened, about 1 minute. Press the Cancel button.

Remove the lime leaves and discard. Swirl the reserved coconut cream into the pot. Serve, garnished with the peanuts and cilantro.

1 small kabocha squash (about 3 lb/1.4 kg), peeled and seeded

2 tablespoons canola oil

3 lb (1.4 kg) boneless beef chuck roast, excess fat trimmed, cut into 1½-inch (4-cm) pieces

Kosher salt and black pepper

1 yellow onion, sliced through root end

1–3 tablespoons massaman curry paste

1 can (13.5 fl oz/400 ml) coconut milk

1½ teaspoons tamarind paste

6 Thai lime leaves

2 tablespoons cornstarch

2 tablespoons cold water

½ cup (90 g) roughly chopped roasted peanuts

¼ cup (15 g) chopped fresh cilantro

For more greenery, add
a handful or two of fresh
spinach to the pot with the
broccoli and toss with tongs.

# Thai Basil Noodles with Beef

Put down that to-go menu and make your own pad Thai with this super-quick one-pot recipe. Look for rice noodles that are about the width of fettuccine noodles where Asian ingredients are sold. Thinner "pad Thai" noodles tend to overcook under pressure.

### SERVES 4

Put the oil in the Instant Pot®, select Sauté, and adjust to More/High heat. Season the beef all over with pepper. When the oil is hot, add half of the beef and cook, stirring frequently, until just browned, about 1 minute. Add the remaining beef, the carrot, and garlic and cook, stirring frequently, for 1 minute. Press the Cancel button.

Add the 1 cup (240 ml) cold water, the stock, and lime leaves (if using), stirring with a wooden spoon to scrape up any browned bits. In a small bowl, stir together the brown sugar, fish sauce, tamarind paste, and sambal oelek and pour over the beef mixture. Place the noodles on top of the beef mixture, pushing them down a bit so they are partially submerged. Place the bell pepper on top but don't stir.

Lock the lid in place and turn the valve to Sealing. Press the Pressure Cook button and set the cook time for 2 minutes at high pressure.

Meanwhile, in a microwave-safe bowl, combine the broccoli and the remaining 2 tablespoons cold water. Cover and microwave on High until crisp-tender, about 3 minutes. Drain and set aside, uncovered.

When the cooking time is up, turn the valve to Venting to quick-release the steam. Carefully remove the lid. Add the broccoli to the pot and toss with tongs. Cover with the lid and let the noodles stand with the Instant Pot® off for 3 minutes to allow them to absorb the sauce and finish cooking. Remove the lime leaves and discard. Serve, garnished with the peanuts and basil.

1 tablespoon canola oil

¾ lb (340 g) sirloin steak, sliced across the grain into strips ¼ inch (6 mm) thick

Freshly ground black pepper

1 large carrot, peeled and thinly sliced

3 cloves garlic, chopped

1 cup (240 ml) plus 2 tablespoons cold water

1 cup (240 ml) chicken stock (page 116 or store-bought)

4 Thai lime leaves (optional)

3 tablespoons firmly packed light brown sugar

3 tablespoons fish sauce or low-sodium soy sauce

2 teaspoons tamarind paste

1 teaspoon–1 tablespoon sambal oelek (Indonesian red chile paste), to taste

½ lb (225 g) wide (⅜ inch/ 1 cm) dried Thai rice noodles

1 red bell pepper, seeded and sliced

4 oz (115 g) broccoli crowns, cut into florets

½ cup (90 g) roughly chopped roasted peanuts

½ cup (15 g) fresh basil leaves

# Barbecue Brisket with Carrots & Parsnips

Brisket needs to braise in the oven for at least 3 hours to become irresistibly succulent, but in the Instant Pot®, it's ready in 1½ hours, with buttery carrots and parsnips cooked in a foil packet at the same time. Be sure to cut the veggies into thick sticks and wrap them tightly in the foil so they don't overcook.

**SERVES 4–6**

Put the 1 tablespoon olive oil in the Instant Pot®, select Sauté, and adjust to More/High heat. Rub the beef all over with the chili powder and season with salt and pepper. When the oil is hot, working in batches if needed, brown the beef on two flat sides, about 3 minutes per side; add more oil between batches if needed. Transfer to a plate. Add the beer to the pot, stirring with a wooden spoon to scrape up any browned bits. Press the Cancel button. Add the onion, ¼ cup (60 g) of the ketchup, and the garlic to the pot and stir to combine. Add the beef in a single layer.

Put the carrots, parsnips, butter, and thyme in the center of a 12-inch (30-cm) length of foil, and season with salt and pepper. Fold up the sides and seal to form a tight packet. Place the packet directly on top of the brisket.

Lock the lid in place and turn the valve to Sealing. Press the Pressure Cook button and set the cook time for 1 hour and 30 minutes at high pressure.

When the cooking time is up, let the steam release naturally for 20 minutes, then turn the valve to Venting to quick-release any residual steam. Carefully remove the lid and transfer the foil packet to a serving bowl but keep it sealed. Transfer the brisket to a cutting board and tent with foil.

Pour 1 cup (240 ml) of the cooking liquid into a fat separator and pour off the fat. Alternatively, pour the 1 cup (240 ml) liquid into a large glass measuring cup, spoon off the fat, and discard. In a bowl, whisk together ½ cup (120 ml) of the defatted cooking liquid, the remaining ketchup, the honey, Worcestershire sauce, sesame oil, and mustard. Thinly slice the brisket across the grain, transfer to a platter, and top with the sauce. Remove the vegetables from the foil and serve alongside.

1 tablespoon olive oil, plus more as needed

1 flat-cut beef brisket (2½–3 lb/1.1–1.4 kg), cut crosswise into 2 pieces

1 tablespoon chili powder

Kosher salt and black pepper

¼ cup (60 ml) lager beer

1 cup (115 g) chopped yellow onion

¾ cup (175 g) ketchup, at room temperature

3 cloves garlic, chopped

3 large carrots, peeled and cut into pieces 3 inches (7.5 cm) long and ½ inch (12 mm) thick

2 parsnips, peeled and cut into pieces 3 inches (7.5 cm) long and ½ inch (12 mm) thick

2 tablespoons unsalted butter

1 teaspoon chopped fresh thyme or ¼ teaspoon dried thyme

¼ cup (90 g) honey

2 tablespoons Worcestershire sauce

1 tablespoon toasted sesame oil

1 tablespoon Dijon mustard

# Beef Tips & Gravy with Chive Whipped Potatoes

Petite sirloin steaks, or tip steaks, are a great value, have tons of beefy flavor, and become fork-tender after just 10 minutes in the Instant Pot®. Don't use a tougher cut like stew meat or chuck roast, or the timing will be off. The whipped potatoes are cooked at the same time using the pot-in-pot method (see page 17).

**SERVES 4**

Put the oil in the Instant Pot®, select Sauté, and adjust to More/High heat. Season the beef with salt and pepper. When the oil is hot, add one handful of the beef and cook without stirring until well browned, about 4 minutes, then stir and continue to cook for 3 minutes longer. Using a slotted spoon, transfer to a plate. Add the onion to the pot and cook, stirring frequently, until beginning to brown, about 6 minutes. Press the Cancel button. Add the stock, Worcestershire sauce, ketchup, garlic powder, ginger, and bay leaf, stirring with a wooden spoon to scrape up any browned bits. Add all of the beef and stir to combine. Place the carrots on top but don't stir.

Place a trivet with tall (2-inch/5-cm) feet in the pot over the beef mixture. In a 7-inch (18-cm) round metal pan with a 6-cup (1.4-L) capacity, combine the potatoes and ½ cup (120 ml) of the cold water and season with salt. Cover tightly with aluminum foil and place on the trivet.

Lock the lid in place and turn the valve to Sealing. Press the Pressure Cook button and set the cook time for 10 minutes at high pressure.

When the cooking time is up, turn the valve to Venting to quick-release the steam. Carefully remove the lid and remove the pan and trivet. Drain the potatoes and transfer to a bowl. Add the butter and whip with a hand-held mixer or mash with a potato masher until smooth. Stir in the cream and chives, and season to taste with salt and pepper. Cover to keep warm.

Using a slotted spoon, transfer the beef and carrots to a large serving bowl and cover to keep warm. In a small bowl, stir together the cornstarch and 2 tablespoons cold water. Add to the pot, select Sauté, and adjust to More/High heat. Simmer until the gravy has thickened, about 1 minute. Pour the gravy over the beef and carrots and serve with the whipped potatoes.

**2 tablespoons olive oil**

**2 lb (1 kg) petite sirloin steaks, cut into 1-inch (2.5-cm) pieces**

**Kosher salt and black pepper**

**1 yellow onion, sliced through root end**

**½ cup (120 ml) chicken stock (page 116 or store-bought)**

**2 tablespoons Worcestershire sauce**

**2 tablespoons ketchup**

**1 teaspoon garlic powder**

**½ teaspoon ground ginger**

**1 bay leaf**

**5 large carrots, peeled and cut into 1-inch (2.5-cm) pieces**

**2 russet potatoes (about ¾ lb/340 g each), cut into 1-inch (2.5-cm) pieces**

**½ cup (120 ml) plus 2 tablespoons cold water**

**3 tablespoons unsalted butter, at room temperature**

**¼–½ cup (60–120 ml) heavy cream or whole milk, warmed**

**2 tablespoons minced fresh chives**

**2 tablespoons cornstarch**

# Pizza-Stuffed Bell Peppers

This recipe features all the awesomeness of pizza, stuffed into a bell pepper, for a weeknight meal that's ready in no time. The raw ground beef is cooked directly in the pepper without being browned first, so use very lean ground beef (5% fat or less) or the peppers will be too greasy.

**SERVES 4**

In a large bowl, stir together the tomato sauce, stock, Italian seasoning, and garlic powder, and season with salt and pepper. Pour 1 cup (240 ml) plus 2 tablespoons of this mixture into the pot. Place a steam rack/trivet with handles in the pot.

Add the ground beef, ½ cup (60 g) of the cheese, the bread crumbs, olives, fennel seeds, and ½ teaspoon each salt and pepper to the remaining tomato sauce in the large bowl.

Cut ½ inch (12 mm) off the top of each bell pepper; reserve the tops. Scoop out the seeds and inner membranes. Finely chop the tops, discarding the stems, and add to the meat and sauce mixture in the large bowl. Add the pepperoni slices and stir until everything is thoroughly combined. Spoon the mixture into the peppers and place them upright on the trivet. Gently press the remaining ½ cup (60 g) cheese onto the filling.

Lock the lid in place and turn the valve to Sealing. Press the Pressure Cook button and set the cook time for 10 minutes at high pressure.

When the cooking time is up, turn the valve to Venting to quick-release the steam. Carefully remove the lid. Using tongs and a large spoon, gently remove the peppers from the pot; they will be very tender. Remove the trivet and stir the sauce in the pot. Spoon the sauce over the peppers and serve right away.

**1 cup (240 ml) canned tomato sauce**

**½ cup (120 ml) chicken stock (page 116 or store-bought)**

**1½ teaspoons dried Italian seasoning**

**1 teaspoon garlic powder**

**Kosher salt and black pepper**

**1 lb (450 g) 95% lean ground beef**

**1 cup (120 g) shredded mozzarella cheese**

**½ cup (50 g) Italian-style dried bread crumbs**

**1 can (2.25 oz/64 g) sliced black olives, drained**

**1 teaspoon fennel seeds**

**4 bell peppers of different colors**

**2 oz (60 g) sliced pepperoni**

*Be careful when topping the peppers with the mozzarella cheese; any that falls off may burn on the bottom of the pot. It's best to gently press the cheese onto the meat filling.*

# Gnocchi Bolognese

The Instant Pot® has a way of making a simple tomato sauce taste like it's been simmering for hours. This meaty version gets extra oomph from umami-rich dried porcini mushrooms, but they're optional if your family doesn't care for fungi. Shelf-stable gnocchi need only a quick heat-up right in the sauce. Look for them in Cryovac packages where dried pasta is sold.

**SERVES 4**

Put the oil in the Instant Pot®, select Sauté, and adjust to More/High heat. When the oil is hot, add the ground beef and cook, breaking up the meat into 2-inch (5-cm) chunks with a spatula, until browned, about 4 minutes. Add the onion, carrot, celery, and Italian seasoning and cook, stirring occasionally, until the onions are tender, about 4 minutes. Add the tomato paste and garlic and cook until fragrant, about 45 seconds. Press the Cancel button.

Add the stock to the pot, stirring with a wooden spoon to scrape up any browned bits. Add the tomatoes and mushrooms (if using) and stir to combine.

Lock the lid in place and turn the valve to Sealing. Press the Pressure Cook button and set the cook time for 15 minutes at high pressure.

When the cooking time is up, turn the valve to Venting to quick-release the steam. Carefully remove the lid. Season the sauce to taste with salt and pepper. Add the gnocchi, breaking up any clumped gnocchi with your fingers, and stir gently to combine. Select Sauté, adjust to Less/Low heat, and cook, stirring only once, until the sauce is bubbly and the gnocchi are heated through, about 5 minutes. Sprinkle with the cheese and serve.

**TIP** *If you'd prefer a lower-carb version (and an extra serving of vegetables), replace the potato gnocchi with frozen cauliflower-based gnocchi and simmer for 3 minutes longer at the end.*

2 tablespoons olive oil

¾ lb (340 g) 90% lean ground beef

1 yellow onion, finely chopped

1 large carrot, peeled and finely chopped

1 rib celery, finely chopped

2 teaspoons dried Italian seasoning

2 tablespoons tomato paste

3 cloves garlic, chopped

½ cup (120 ml) beef or chicken stock (pages 116–117 or store-bought)

2 cups (500 g) canned crushed tomatoes with basil

½ oz (15 g) dried porcini mushrooms (optional)

Kosher salt and black pepper

1 package (16 oz/453 g) shelf-stable potato gnocchi

½ cup (60 g) grated Parmesan cheese

# Beef Barley Soup

A rich beef broth studded with veggies and nutrient-packed barley is the perfect winter warmer. Dried porcini mushrooms and soy sauce amp up the beefy flavor. This soup can be held with the Keep Warm function for hours, so it's ideal on busy nights when you're feeding family members at different times.

**SERVES 6**

Put 1 tablespoon of the oil in the Instant Pot®, select Sauté, and adjust to More/High heat. Season the beef with 1 teaspoon salt and ½ teaspoon pepper. When the oil is hot, add one handful of the beef and cook, stirring occasionally, until well browned, about 8 minutes. Transfer to a plate. (There's no need to brown the rest of the beef.)

Add the remaining 1 tablespoon oil, the onion, carrots, and celery to the pot and cook, stirring frequently, until the onions are tender, about 4 minutes. Add the garlic, tomato paste, rosemary, and thyme and cook, stirring occasionally, until fragrant, about 1 minute. Add the wine and simmer, stirring with a wooden spoon to scrape up any browned bits, until nearly evaporated, about 1 minute. Press the Cancel button. Add all of the beef, the stocks, barley, mushrooms, and bay leaf to the pot.

Lock the lid in place and turn the valve to Sealing. Press the Pressure Cook button and set the cook time for 30 minutes at high pressure.

When the cooking time is up, let the steam release naturally for 10 minutes, then turn the valve to Venting to quick-release any residual steam. Carefully remove the lid and remove the bay leaf and discard. Season to taste with soy sauce.

Ladle the soup into bowls and serve.

**2 tablespoons olive oil**

**2 lb (1 kg) boneless beef chuck roast, excess fat trimmed, meat cut into 1-inch (2.5-cm) pieces**

**Kosher salt and black pepper**

**1 yellow onion, chopped**

**3 carrots, peeled and sliced**

**2 ribs celery, sliced**

**3 cloves garlic, chopped**

**1 tablespoon tomato paste**

**1½ teaspoons chopped fresh rosemary**

**1 teaspoon dried thyme**

**½ cup (120 ml) dry red wine**

**3 cups (700 ml) beef stock (page 117 or store-bought)**

**2 cups (475 ml) chicken stock (page 116 or store-bought)**

**¾ cup (150 g) pearl barley**

**½ ounce (15 g) dried porcini mushrooms**

**1 bay leaf**

**Low-sodium soy sauce**

*Add a green garnish with roughly chopped cilantro or fresh flat-leaf parsley, chopped green onions, or diced fresh or pickled jalapeño.*

# Two-Bean No-Soak Beef Chili

This recipe for hearty chili saves money and time because dried beans (no soaking required!) are cooked at the same time as juicy chunks of beef. The trick? Cook the chili without the tomato paste and then add it at the end, as the acidity would otherwise prevent the beans from cooking effectively. Keep in mind that chili powder blends vary; taste yours before adding it to the chili and adjust the quantity based on your family's tolerance for spicy food.

**SERVES 6–8**

Put the oil in the Instant Pot®, select Sauté, and adjust to More/High heat. Season the beef all over with salt and pepper. When the oil is hot, add one small handful of the beef. Cook, stirring frequently, until the beef is well browned, about 4 minutes. Add the onion and cook, stirring frequently, until tender, about 4 minutes. Add the garlic, chili powder, and cumin and cook until fragrant, about 30 seconds. Add the stock, stirring with a wooden spoon to scrape up any browned bits. Press the Cancel button. Add the remaining beef, the black beans, pinto beans, and bell pepper and stir to combine.

Lock the lid in place and turn the valve to Sealing. Press the Pressure Cook button and set the cook time for 25 minutes at high pressure.

When the cooking time is up, let the steam release naturally for 15 minutes, then turn the valve to Venting to quick-release any residual steam. Carefully remove the lid.

In a small bowl, whisk together the tomato paste and 1 cup (240 ml) of the cooking liquid. Add to the pot, select Sauté, and adjust to Normal/Medium heat. Simmer uncovered, stirring gently so you don't break up the tender beef too much, until the flavors have melded, about 5 minutes. Season to taste with salt and pepper. Sprinkle with the cheese and serve.

**2 tablespoons olive oil**

**2 lb (1 kg) boneless beef chuck roast, excess fat trimmed, cut into 1½-inch (4-cm) pieces**

**Kosher salt and black pepper**

**1 yellow onion, chopped**

**3 cloves garlic, chopped**

**¼ cup (24 g) mild chili powder**

**1 tablespoon ground cumin**

**4 cups (950 ml) beef or chicken stock (pages 116–117 or store-bought)**

**1 cup (200 g) dried black beans, rinsed and picked over**

**¾ cup (150 g) dried pinto beans, rinsed and picked over**

**1 red or yellow bell pepper, seeded and chopped**

**½ cup (115 g) tomato paste**

**1½ cups (170 g) grated Cheddar cheese**

# Moroccan Meatball Soup
# with Pearl Couscous

This soup is a little spicy and just the right amount of sweet. The spice comes from harissa, a Moroccan chile-and-spice paste sold in tubes or jars. You'll find it at well-stocked grocery stores and online. Pearl couscous (aka Israeli couscous) is a wheat pasta that's about the size of a peppercorn. If you can't find pearl couscous, substitute another small pasta shape, such as ditalini or orzo.

**SERVES 4–6**

In a bowl, combine the ground beef, harissa, ¾ teaspoon salt, and ½ teaspoon pepper. Using your hands or a wooden spoon, stir gently to combine. Form into 20 meatballs, using about 1½ tablespoons for each one. Set aside.

Put the oil in the Instant Pot®, select Sauté, and adjust to More/High heat. When the oil is hot, add the onion and carrots and cook, stirring frequently, until the onions are tender, about 4 minutes. Add the garlic and cook until fragrant, about 30 seconds. Add the stock, stirring with a wooden spoon to scrape up any browned bits. Press the Cancel button.

Add the chickpeas, tomatoes, couscous, dates, ginger, cumin, and cinnamon stick to the pot and stir to combine. Add the meatballs but don't stir.

Lock the lid in place and turn the valve to Sealing. Press the Pressure Cook button and set the cook time for 12 minutes at high pressure.

When the cooking time is up, let the steam release naturally for 10 minutes, then turn the valve to Venting to quick-release any residual steam. Carefully remove the lid. Remove the cinnamon stick and discard. Stir in the lemon juice and season to taste with salt and pepper.

Ladle the soup into bowls and serve with the remaining harissa on the side for anyone who wants a tad more heat.

**TIP** *Don't be tempted to skip the harissa; the flavorful blend of ground chiles, cumin, caraway, and garlic is much more than just hot.*

1 lb (450 g) 90% lean ground beef or lamb

2 teaspoons–1½ tablespoons harissa paste, plus more to taste

Kosher salt and black pepper

1 tablespoon olive oil

1 yellow onion, chopped

2 carrots, peeled and sliced ¼ inch (6 mm) thick

2 large cloves garlic, minced

4 cups (950 ml) chicken stock (page 116 or store-bought)

1 can (15 oz/425 g) chickpeas, rinsed and drained

1½ cups (375 g) canned crushed tomatoes

½ cup (70 g) pearl couscous

2 medjool dates, pitted and chopped

1½ teaspoons ground ginger

1½ teaspoons ground cumin

1 cinnamon stick

2 tablespoons fresh lemon juice

# Cheeseburger One-Pot Pasta

This hearty one-pot pasta dish is both familiar and fun—and it really does taste just like a juicy cheeseburger! Serve as is or drizzle with extra ketchup for the ketchup-crazy in your family. Be sure to use lean ground beef so you don't have to drain off the fat after browning the meat. Leaving the beef in large chunks will result in a better, meatball-like texture.

**SERVES 4**

Put the oil in the Instant Pot®, select Sauté, and adjust to More/High heat. When the oil is hot, add the ground beef and onion and cook, breaking up the meat into 1-inch (2.5-cm) chunks with a spatula, until the beef is browned, about 5 minutes. Press the Cancel button.

Add 3 cups (700 ml) water, ketchup, pickle juice, mustard, onion powder, paprika, garlic powder, ¾ teaspoon salt, and ¼ teaspoon pepper to the pot, stirring with a wooden spoon to scrape up any browned bits. Add the pasta and toss to coat.

Lock the lid in place and turn the valve to Sealing. Press the Pressure Cook button and set the cook time for 5 minutes at low pressure.

When the cooking time is up, turn the valve to Venting to quick-release the steam. Carefully remove the lid. Add half of the Cheddar and all of the cream cheese and stir with a rubber spatula until the cheese has melted. Sprinkle with the remaining Cheddar and the pickles and serve.

1 tablespoon olive oil

1 lb (450g) 95% lean ground beef

1 yellow onion, chopped

¼ cup (60 g) ketchup

2 tablespoons pickle juice from jarred hamburger pickle slices

1 tablespoon yellow or Dijon mustard

1 teaspoon onion powder

1 teaspoon sweet paprika

½ teaspoon garlic powder

Kosher salt and black pepper

¾ lb (340 g) dried rotini pasta

1½ cups (170 g) finely grated Cheddar or Cheddar-Colby blend

¼ cup (40 g) whipped cream cheese

½ cup (170 g) roughly chopped hamburger pickle slices

The peas are optional in this filling dish (in case you have any pea haters in the family). For a more intense curry flavor, add an additional tablespoon of the curry paste.

# Indian Spiced Beef with Peas & Basmati Rice

This thrifty ground beef dish, called *keema* in India, is typically served with rice but is also delicious tucked inside squishy hamburger buns, sloppy joe–style. The usual long list of spices is streamlined here by swapping in thick Indian curry paste, available in jars where Indian ingredients are sold. Don't use diluted curry-flavored simmer sauces, as they're too thin for this recipe.

## SERVES 4

Put the butter in the Instant Pot®, select Sauté, and adjust to More/High heat. When the butter is hot, add the onion and cook, stirring frequently, until beginning to brown, about 5 minutes. Add the ground beef, ginger, and garlic and cook, breaking up the meat into large 1-inch (2.5-cm) chunks with a spatula, until beginning to brown, about 5 minutes. (Keeping the meat in larger pieces will add texture to the dish.) Press the Cancel button. Add the tomatoes, ¼ cup (60 ml) of the stock, the curry paste, and cinnamon stick, stirring with a wooden spoon to scrape up any browned bits.

Place a trivet with tall (2-inch/5-cm) feet in the pot over the beef mixture. In a 7-inch (18-cm) round metal pan with a 6-cup (1.4-L) capacity, stir together the rice and the remaining 1¼ cups (300 ml) stock. Cover tightly with aluminum foil and place on the trivet.

Lock the lid in place and turn the valve to Sealing. Press the Pressure Cook button and set the cook time for 6 minutes at high pressure.

When the cooking time is up, let the steam release naturally for 5 minutes, then turn the valve to Venting to quick-release any residual steam. Carefully remove the lid and remove the pan and trivet. Fluff the rice with a fork.

Remove the cinnamon stick from the meat mixture and discard. Stir in the peas (if using) and garam masala, select Sauté, and adjust to More/High heat. Simmer until the peas are heated through, about 1 minute. Serve with the rice.

- 1 tablespoon unsalted butter
- 1 yellow onion, finely chopped
- 1 lb (450 g) 90% lean ground beef or lamb
- 1 tablespoon peeled and minced fresh ginger
- 3 cloves garlic, chopped
- ½ cup (100 g) drained canned diced plum tomatoes
- 1½ cups (360 ml) chicken stock (page 116 or store-bought)
- 2 tablespoons mild Indian curry paste (such as Patak's)
- 1 cinnamon stick
- 1¼ cups (245 g) basmati rice, rinsed and drained
- 1 cup (140 g) frozen peas, thawed (optional)
- 1½ teaspoons garam masala (Indian spice blend)

Maple-Mustard Pork Chops
with Sweet Potatoes
(page 83)

# PORK

Can't find boneless country-style ribs? Use a pork butt roast instead and cut it into 1½-by-1-inch (4-by-2.5-cm) strips, then cut them crosswise into chunks.

# Pork Verde & Pinto Bean Tostadas

This easy tomatillo pork dish becomes fork-tender in just 20 minutes under high pressure, thanks to convenient boneless country-style pork ribs. It's wonderful on tostadas, but you can also serve it as a stew with steamed rice, or tuck the meat and beans into tortillas for delicious tacos.

### SERVES 6

Put the oil in the Instant Pot®, select Sauté, and adjust to More/High heat. In a large bowl, stir together the cumin, coriander, 1 teaspoon salt, and ½ teaspoon pepper. Add the pork and toss to coat. When the oil is hot, add one handful of the pork and cook, stirring occasionally, until well browned, about 5 minutes. Press the Cancel button.

Add the salsa to the pot, stirring with a wooden spoon to scrape up any browned bits. Add the remaining pork, the onion, garlic, and oregano and stir to combine.

Lock the lid in place and turn the valve to Sealing. Press the Pressure Cook button and set the cook time for 20 minutes at high pressure.

When the cooking time is up, let the steam release naturally for 10 minutes, then turn the valve to Venting to quick-release any residual steam. Carefully remove the lid. Using a slotted spoon, transfer the pork to a medium bowl and spoon ½ cup (120 ml) of the solids and cooking liquid over the pork. (Save the remaining cooking liquid for a base for chili, if desired.) Add the cilantro, lime zest, and lime juice to the bowl and stir to combine.

Spread the refried beans on the tostada shells. Top with the pork, cheese, lettuce, and a dollop of sour cream. Serve right away.

1 tablespoon olive oil

1 tablespoon ground cumin

1 tablespoon ground coriander

Kosher salt and black pepper

3 lb (1.4 kg) boneless country-style pork ribs, cut into 1½-inch (4-cm) pieces

1 cup (240 ml) thin, mild green salsa, such as Herdez

1 yellow onion, sliced through root end

4 cloves garlic, chopped

2 teaspoons dried Mexican oregano

¼ cup (15 g) chopped fresh cilantro

Zest and juice of 1 lime

1 can (15 oz/425 g) refried pinto beans, warmed

12 tostada shells

1½ cups (170 g) grated Cheddar cheese

4 cups (140 g) shredded romaine lettuce

¾ cup (170 g) sour cream

# Spanish Pork Tenderloin with Potatoes

Pork tenderloin cooks to perfection in the same amount of time as fun multicolored fingerling potatoes in this one-pot meal. Piquillo peppers, sold in jars, are slightly smoky sweet red peppers used in Spanish cooking. If you can't find them, use roasted red bell peppers instead.

**SERVES 4**

Put the oil in the Instant Pot®, select Sauté, and adjust to More/High heat. Season the pork all over with salt and pepper. When the oil is hot, brown the pork on all sides, about 5 minutes total.

Add the onion to the pot and cook, stirring frequently, until tender, about 4 minutes. Add the garlic and cook until fragrant, about 30 seconds. Add the sherry and simmer, stirring with a wooden spoon to scrape up any browned bits. Press the Cancel button. Stir in the stock, piquillo peppers, thyme, paprika, and potatoes, and season with salt and pepper. Add the pork and any accumulated juices to the pot.

Lock the lid in place and turn the valve to Sealing. Press the Pressure Cook button and set the cook time for 4 minutes at high pressure.

When the cooking time is up, let the steam release naturally for 15 minutes, then turn the valve to Venting to quick-release any residual steam. Carefully remove the lid. Check the pork for doneness; an instant-read thermometer inserted into the center should register 140°F (60°C). If the pork is not done, cover with a regular pan lid and let the pork stand in the pot for a few minutes longer; the residual heat will finish cooking the meat.

Transfer the pork to a cutting board. Cut into slices 1 inch (2.5 cm) thick and arrange on a serving platter. Using a slotted spoon, transfer the potatoes and peppers to the platter and tent with aluminum foil.

In a small bowl, stir together the cornstarch and cold water. Add to the pot, select Sauté, and adjust to Normal/Medium heat. Simmer until the sauce thickens, about 2 minutes. Pour the sauce over the pork and serve.

1 tablespoon olive oil

2 pork tenderloins (about 1 lb/450 g each)

Kosher salt and black pepper

1 small yellow onion, sliced through root end

3 cloves garlic, minced

¼ cup (60 ml) dry sherry or white wine

¼ cup (60 ml) chicken stock (page 116 or store-bought)

½ cup (90 g) sliced roasted piquillo or red bell peppers

2 teaspoons chopped fresh thyme or ½ teaspoon dried thyme

¼ teaspoon smoked paprika

1½ lb (680 g) multicolored fingerling potatoes, halved lengthwise

1½ teaspoons cornstarch

1 tablespoon cold water

# Pork Lo Mein

These are just like takeout noodles but faster and healthier. The vegetables and pork will cook along with the dry noodles in just 2 minutes under high pressure. Look for thin wheat noodles, called lo mein (not fried noodles), in Asian markets or online.

**SERVES 4**

In a small bowl, stir together the stock, soy sauce, and rice cooking wine; set aside.

Put the oil in the Instant Pot®, select Sauté, and adjust to More/High heat. Cut the pork crosswise into 2 pieces then rub all over with the five-spice powder and season with salt and pepper. When the oil is hot, brown the pork all over for about 5 minutes total. Transfer to a cutting board and cut crosswise into ½-inch (12-mm) slices, and then into 1–1½-inch (2.5–4-cm) pieces; set aside.

Add the bell pepper, onion, mushrooms, and baby corn to the pot and cook, stirring frequently, until the onion begins to brown, about 5 minutes. Add the garlic and cook until fragrant, about 30 seconds. Press the Cancel button.

Add the stock mixture, stirring with a wooden spoon to scrape up any browned bits. Return the pork to the pot and stir to combine. Break the noodles into 3-inch (7.5-cm) lengths and scatter over the pork and vegetables. Gently press down on the noodles to partially submerge them but don't stir.

Lock the lid in place and turn the valve to Sealing. Press the Pressure Cook button and set the cook time for 2 minutes at high pressure.

When the cooking time is up, turn the valve to Venting to quick-release the steam. Carefully remove the lid. Add the hoisin sauce and green onions, stir gently (some noodles may not be completely cooked), and cover with the lid. Let stand for 2–3 minutes to finish cooking the noodles. Serve right away.

½ cup (120 ml) plus 2 tablespoons chicken stock (page 116 or store-bought)

3 tablespoons low-sodium soy sauce

2 tablespoons rice cooking wine or dry sherry

2 tablespoons canola oil

1 pork tenderloin (about 1 lb/450 g)

1 teaspoon Chinese five-spice powder

Kosher salt and black pepper

1 small red bell pepper, seeded and sliced

½ yellow onion, thinly sliced

5 shiitake mushrooms, stemmed and brushed clean, caps thickly sliced

1 can (15 oz/425 g) baby corn, drained and cut into bite-size pieces

4 cloves garlic, thinly sliced

6 oz (170 g) dried lo mein or chow mein noodles

2 tablespoons hoisin sauce

3 green onions, thinly sliced

# Pork Loin with Cornbread Dressing & Apple Cider Gravy

Pork loin (not to be confused with the smaller pork tenderloin) becomes delectably moist and juicy in the Instant Pot®. In this ode to the flavors of autumn, the meat is cooked with an apple-studded cornbread dressing and the cooking liquid includes apple cider, which becomes a delicious sweet-savory gravy. Serve with roasted butternut squash or a green salad.

**SERVES 6**

Put 1 tablespoon of the oil in the Instant Pot®, select Sauté, and adjust to More/High heat. Season the pork all over with salt and pepper and 1 tablespoon of the poultry seasoning. When the oil is hot, brown the roast on all sides, about 8 minutes total. Transfer to a plate.

Add the remaining 1 tablespoon oil, the onion, and celery to the pot and cook, stirring frequently, until the onion is tender, about 4 minutes. Add the garlic and remaining 1 tablespoon poultry seasoning and cook until fragrant, about 30 seconds. Add the stock, stirring with a wooden spoon to scrape up any browned bits. Press the Cancel button.

Transfer the stock mixture to a large bowl. Add the cornbread, apple, and parsley and stir until moistened. Spoon the dressing into a 7-inch (18-cm) round metal pan with a 6-cup (1.4-L) capacity. Cover tightly with aluminum foil. Alternatively, put the dressing on a piece of aluminum foil; fold up the sides of the foil and seal to form a tight packet that will fit in the pot.

**2 tablespoons olive oil**

**1 pork loin roast (about 3 lb/1.4 kg)**

**Kosher salt and black pepper**

**2 tablespoons poultry seasoning or dried sage**

**1 yellow onion, chopped**

**3 ribs celery, chopped**

**2 cloves garlic, chopped**

**½ cup (120 ml) chicken stock (page 116 or store-bought)**

**14 oz (400 g) day-old cornbread, crumbled into 1-inch (2.5-cm) pieces**

**1 Granny Smith apple, peeled, cored, and finely chopped**

**2 tablespoons chopped fresh flat-leaf parsley**

*continued on page 72*

*continued from page 70*

Return the roast to the pot and pour the apple cider over the meat. Place the pan (or foil packet) with the dressing directly on top of the roast.

Lock the lid in place and turn the valve to Sealing. Press the Pressure Cook button and set the cook time for 30 minutes at high pressure.

When the cooking time is up, let the steam release naturally for 10 minutes, then turn the valve to Venting to quick-release any residual steam. Carefully remove the lid, remove the dressing from the pot, and set the dressing aside, covered.

Check the pork for doneness; an instant-read thermometer inserted into the center should register 140°F (60°C). If the pork is not done, select Sauté, adjust to More/High heat, and place a regular pan lid on the pot. Simmer until the roast reaches 140°F, about 5 minutes longer. Transfer the roast to a cutting board and tent with foil.

In a small bowl, stir together the butter and flour until smooth. Select Sauté, adjust to Normal/Medium heat, and bring the cooking liquid to a simmer. Gradually add the butter-flour mixture, whisking frequently, and cook until the gravy is thick and bubbly, about 2 minutes. Season to taste with salt and pepper.

Thinly slice the roast and serve with the dressing and gravy.

¾ **cup (180 ml) apple cider**

**2 tablespoons unsalted butter, at room temperature**

**2 tablespoons all-purpose flour**

# Sticky Hoisin Baby Back Ribs

These tender ribs get a quick dry rub and a delicious Asian-inspired hoisin glaze before being cooked for just 25 minutes. For a get-ahead dinner, cook the ribs in the Instant Pot® in advance and refrigerate them for up to 3 days and then reheat them on the grill or under the broiler before serving (see Tip).

### SERVES 4

Place the ribs on a baking sheet. In a small bowl, stir together the garlic powder, brown sugar, mustard, ginger, and 2 teaspoons salt. Rub the mixture all over the ribs, particularly the meaty sides. Let stand at room temperature for 1 hour, or cover and refrigerate for up to 24 hours.

In a small bowl, stir together the hoisin sauce, ketchup, and sesame oil. Brush the ribs with a few tablespoons of the sauce, just to lightly coat them; set the remaining sauce aside. Place the ribs in the Instant Pot®, standing them upright against the sides. (You may need to cut the racks into smaller portions to fit them in the pot.) Pour the water into the pot.

Lock the lid in place and turn the valve to Sealing. Press the Pressure Cook button and set the cook time for 25 minutes at high pressure.

Meanwhile, in a small saucepan over medium heat, bring the remaining sauce to a simmer. Remove from the heat.

When the cooking time is up, turn the valve to Venting to quick-release the steam. Carefully remove the lid. Transfer the ribs to a large platter, spoon the warm sauce over them, and sprinkle with the green onions and sesame seeds. Cut into individual ribs and serve.

**2 racks baby back pork ribs (about 3 lb/1.4 kg each)**

**1 tablespoon garlic powder**

**1 tablespoon firmly packed light brown sugar**

**2 teaspoons dry mustard**

**2 teaspoons ground ginger**

**Kosher salt**

**½ cup (120 g) hoisin sauce**

**½ cup (115 g) ketchup**

**1 teaspoon toasted sesame oil**

**½ cup (120 ml) water**

**4 green onions, finely chopped**

**2 tablespoons toasted sesame seeds**

**TIP** *To grill the cooked ribs, brush them with some of the remaining sauce and grill over direct, medium-high heat until charred on the edges, 4 minutes if just out of the pot, 10 minutes if made ahead and refrigerated. Alternatively, broil the ribs on a foil-lined baking sheet about 4 inches (10 cm) from the broiler element until the edges are charred, 2 minutes if just out of the pot, or 6 inches (15 cm) away from the broiler element until heated through, about 10 minutes, if cold. Brush again with the sauce and serve.*

If using eggs straight from the refrigerator, place the unbroken eggs in a bowl of hot tap water while the pasta cooks to help warm them slightly before cracking them into the serving bowl.

# Carbonara Pasta with Swiss Chard

Creamy and decadent but with a healthy dose of greens, this updated Roman pasta is a breeze to make in the Instant Pot®. The bacon contributes smoky flavor, the Swiss chard adds a veggie, and the eggs become a quick, silky-rich sauce for this one-pot family meal.

## SERVES 4

Put the oil in the Instant Pot®, select Sauté, and adjust to Normal/Medium heat. When the oil is hot, add the bacon and cook, stirring occasionally, until crisp and browned, 4–5 minutes. Add the garlic and cook until fragrant, about 45 seconds. Add the chard and cook, tossing with tongs, until wilted and tender, about 2 minutes. Press the Cancel button. Transfer the bacon-chard mixture to a bowl and cover to keep warm. (It's fine if some of the garlic remains in the pot.)

Add the spaghetti, stock, hot water, ½ teaspoon salt, and several grinds of pepper to the pot and stir to combine, making sure most of the pasta is submerged and is splayed at all angles to reduce clumping.

Lock the lid in place and turn the valve to Sealing. Press the Pressure Cook button and set the cook time for 5 minutes at high pressure.

Meanwhile, in a large serving bowl, whisk together the eggs and cheese; set aside.

When the cooking time is up, turn the valve to Venting to quick-release the steam. Carefully remove the lid. Return the bacon-chard mixture to the pot and toss with tongs to break up any clumps of pasta. Cover with the lid with the Instant Pot® off for 1 minute. Quickly pour the contents of the pot into the bowl with the egg mixture and toss with tongs to coat the pasta. (The eggs will cook from the heat of the pasta.) Season to taste with salt and pepper and serve right away.

3 tablespoons olive oil

3 slices thick-cut bacon, chopped

4 cloves garlic, thinly sliced

½ bunch Swiss chard, thick stems and ribs removed, leaves torn into bite-size pieces (3 cups/130 g)

¾ lb (340 g) spaghetti, broken in half

1¼ cups (300 ml) chicken stock (page 116 or store-bought)

1¼ cups (300 ml) hot water

Kosher salt and black pepper

3 large eggs, at room temperature

½ cup (60 g) grated Parmesan cheese

# Vietnamese Pork Chops & Greens

A quick blender marinade infuses bone-in pork chops with an herby lemongrass and garlic flavor. Chopped lacinato kale stirred into the warm pot right before serving adds a healthy dose of greens. Serve with jasmine rice or vermicelli rice noodles.

**SERVES 4**

In a blender or mini food processor, combine the lemongrass, shallot, brown sugar, fish sauce, soy sauce, garlic, and pepper and process until mostly smooth. Pour into a lock-top plastic bag or a small nonaluminum baking dish just large enough to hold the pork chops in a single layer. Add the chops, toss to coat, and refrigerate for at least 1 hour and up to 8 hours.

Put the oil in the Instant Pot®, select Sauté, and adjust to More/High heat. Remove the pork chops from the marinade, reserving the marinade. Pat the chops dry. When the oil is hot, brown the chops on both sides, 2–3 minutes per side. Transfer to a plate. Press the Cancel button. Pour off the oil from the pot.

Return the pot to the appliance. Add the stock, stirring with a wooden spoon to scrape up any browned bits. Add the reserved marinade and stir to combine. Return the pork chops to the pot.

Lock the lid in place and turn the valve to Sealing. Press the Pressure Cook button and set the cook time for 10 minutes at high pressure.

When the cooking time is up, let the steam release naturally for 10 minutes, then turn the valve to Venting to quick-release any residual steam. Carefully remove the lid.

**2 stalks lemongrass, trimmed and finely chopped (about 6 tablespoons)**

**1 small shallot, sliced (about ¼ cup)**

**3 tablespoons firmly packed light brown sugar**

**3 tablespoons fish sauce**

**3 tablespoons low-sodium soy sauce**

**6 cloves garlic, peeled**

**½ teaspoon freshly ground black pepper**

**4 center-cut, bone-in pork chops (each about ½ lb/ 225 g and 1½ inches/4 cm thick)**

Check the pork for doneness; an instant-read thermometer inserted near (but not touching) the bone should register 140°F (60°C). If the chops are not done, cover them with a regular pan lid, select Sauté, and adjust to Normal/Medium heat. Simmer, turning the chops once, until they are done, 1–5 minutes longer. Transfer the chops to a platter and tent with aluminum foil.

Pour off all but 2 tablespoons of the cooking liquid from the pot and return the pot to the appliance. Select Sauté, adjust to More/High heat, and add the kale. Cook, stirring frequently with tongs, until the kale is tender, about 3 minutes. Transfer to the platter with the pork and serve.

**TIP** *Packaged lemongrass paste is a great time-saver. It's sold in tubes in the produce department of well-stocked grocery stores and will keep for weeks in the fridge. You can also find more fragrant minced lemongrass in plastic jars in the frozen-food section of some Asian markets. It will last for months in the freezer.*

**1 tablespoon safflower or canola oil**

**1 cup (240 ml) chicken stock (page 116 or store-bought)**

**1 bunch lacinato kale, thick stems and ribs removed, leaves chopped**

# Korean Pork Sliders with Asian Pear Slaw

These succulent sliders are not your everyday pulled pork. They feature a zingy, gingery barbecue sauce made with gochujang, the addictive Korean miso–red chile paste. Look for it online and where Asian ingredients are sold. The crunchy slaw boasts a touch of sweetness thanks to an Asian pear, although a medium-firm Bartlett pear makes a fine substitute.

**SERVES 6–12**

To make the pork, put the canola oil in the Instant Pot®, select Sauté, and adjust to More/High heat. Season the pork all over with salt and pepper. When the oil is hot, brown the pork all over, about 3 minutes per side. Transfer to a plate. Add the onion to the pot and cook, stirring frequently, until tender, about 4 minutes. Add the garlic and ginger and cook until fragrant, about 30 seconds. Add ½ cup (120 ml) water and the soy sauce, stirring with a wooden spoon to scrape up any browned bits. Return the pork to the pot. Press the Cancel button.

In a small bowl, stir together the gochujang, ketchup, brown sugar, vinegar, sesame oil, and five-spice powder. Spoon ¼ cup (60 ml) of the mixture over the pork, spreading it evenly on the top of the meat but limiting the amount that drips into the liquid below. Set the remaining gochujang mixture aside.

Lock the lid in place and turn the valve to Sealing. Press the Pressure Cook button and set the cook time for 1 hour and 15 minutes at high pressure for a 4-lb (1.8-kg) roast and 1 hour and 30 minutes for a 5-lb (2.3-kg) roast.

When the cooking time is up, let the steam release naturally for 15 minutes, then turn the valve to Venting to quick-release any residual steam. Carefully remove the lid, transfer the pork to a cutting board, and tent with aluminum foil.

### FOR THE PORK
**2 tablespoons canola oil**

**1 boneless pork butt (4–5 lb/1.8–2.3 kg)**

**Kosher salt and black pepper**

**1 yellow onion, sliced**

**6 cloves garlic, chopped**

**3 tablespoons plus 1 teaspoon peeled and chopped fresh ginger**

**½ cup (120 ml) low-sodium soy sauce**

**½ cup (115 g) gochujang (Korean chile paste)**

**½ cup (115 g) ketchup**

**⅓ cup (80 g) firmly packed light brown sugar**

**2 tablespoons rice vinegar**

**2 tablespoons toasted sesame oil**

**2 teaspoons Chinese five-spice powder**

*continued on page 80*

These flavor-rich and hearty sliders are also terrific for easy entertaining or any game-day menu; pair them with potato salad (page 119) and cold beer.

*continued from page 78*

Pour the cooking liquid into a fat separator and pour off the fat. Alternatively, pour the cooking liquid into a large glass measuring cup, spoon off the fat, and discard. Return 1 cup (240 ml) of the defatted cooking liquid to the pot. Whisk in the reserved gochujang mixture, select Sauté, and adjust to Normal/Medium heat. Cook, stirring frequently, until the sauce is thickened and bubbly, about 5 minutes. Meanwhile, cut the pork into thin slices or shred with 2 forks, discarding most of the fat. (A little fat is okay; it adds flavor.) Return the meat to the pot and stir to combine with the sauce. (The meat can be kept warm, covered, using the Keep Warm function, for up to 3 hours.)

To make the slaw, in a large bowl, toss the cabbage with 1 teaspoon salt, then add the pear, carrot, and green onions. In a small bowl, whisk together the vinegar, canola oil, granulated sugar, ginger, and sesame oil. Add the dressing to the cabbage mixture and toss to combine.

Divide the pork among the slider buns, top with the slaw, and serve.

**TIP** *Despite its name, pork butt comes from the front shoulder area of the pig. It's a fatty cut of meat, so you may wish to trim some of the fat on the outside of the roast before searing it. The fat that runs within the roast adds flavor and will dissolve as it cooks, yielding very tender meat.*

## FOR THE SLAW

**5 cups (425 g) finely shredded green cabbage**

**Kosher salt**

**1 firm Asian pear, cored and cut into matchsticks**

**1 large carrot, peeled and grated**

**2 green onions, thinly sliced**

**¼ cup (60 ml) rice vinegar**

**3 tablespoons canola oil**

**1 tablespoon granulated sugar**

**1 teaspoon peeled and finely grated fresh ginger**

**1 teaspoon toasted sesame oil**

**20–25 slider buns**

# Sausage & Fennel Penne

Fennel is a bulb vegetable with a sweet flavor that pairs well with Italian sausage. Never fear if you have picky eaters; the vegetable melts into the sauce beautifully under pressure. If your fennel still has the feathery fronds attached, chop them and sprinkle over the finished pasta for a lovely green garnish.

## SERVES 4

Put the oil in the Instant Pot®, select Sauté, and adjust to More/High heat. Form the sausage meat into rustic little dabs, about 1 tablespoon each. (No need to roll them into perfect balls.) When the oil is hot, add the sausage and cook without stirring for 2 minutes. Using a spatula, carefully flip the sausage over and cook until golden brown on the second side, about 3 minutes. Transfer to a plate.

Add the onion, sliced fennel, sage, and fennel seeds to the pot and cook, stirring frequently, until the onion and fennel are tender, about 4 minutes. Add the garlic and cook until fragrant, about 30 seconds. Press the Cancel button.

Add the stock, water, and tomato paste, stirring to scrape up any browned bits. Return the sausage to the pot. Add ½ teaspoon each salt and black pepper and the red pepper flakes and stir to combine. Add the pasta and gently press down on the noodles to partially submerge them.

Lock the lid in place and turn the valve to Sealing. Press the Pressure Cook button and set the cook time for 6 minutes at low pressure.

When the cooking time is up, turn the valve to Venting to quick-release the steam. Carefully remove the lid, stir gently, and let stand uncovered for 1–2 minutes to allow the pasta to absorb more of the stock mixture. Season to taste with salt and black pepper. Sprinkle with the cheese and fennel fronds (if using) and serve.

**TIP** *To remove the hard core from the fennel bulb, cut it in half lengthwise, then use a paring knife to cut the solid white triangular-shaped core out of the bottom center of the bulb. Save for stock or discard.*

**2 tablespoons olive oil**

**1 lb (450 g) sweet Italian sausages, casings removed**

**1 yellow onion, chopped**

**1 small fennel bulb, trimmed, cored, and thinly sliced, fronds reserved for garnish (optional)**

**1½ tablespoons minced fresh sage or 1½ teaspoons dried sage**

**1 teaspoon fennel seeds**

**4 cloves garlic, minced**

**2 cups (475 ml) chicken stock (page 116 or store-bought)**

**1 cup (240 ml) water**

**2 tablespoons tomato paste**

**Kosher salt and black pepper**

**Pinch of red pepper flakes**

**¾ lb (340 g) penne pasta**

**½ cup (60 g) grated pecorino romano cheese**

You can substitute another hard vegetable, such as potatoes, carrots, parsnips, or butternut squash, for the sweet potatoes, if you like.

# Maple-Mustard Pork Chops with Sweet Potatoes

Look for thick bone-in chops cut from the center portion of the loin. The best ones will have a "T-bone" with a bit of the lighter loin meat and a section of the tenderloin on them. The side of sweet potatoes cooks at the same time in a steamer basket.

**SERVES 4**

Put the oil in the Instant Pot®, select Sauté, and adjust to Normal/Medium heat. When the oil is hot, add the bacon and cook, stirring occasionally, until crisp and browned, 4–5 minutes. Transfer to a plate.

Season the chops with salt and pepper. Working in batches, brown until golden on one side, 3 minutes per batch. Transfer to a plate. Remove the inner pot, pour off all but 1 tablespoon of the fat, and return the pot to the appliance. Add the onion and cook, stirring, until tender, 4 minutes. Add the sage and garlic and cook until fragrant, 30 seconds. Press the Cancel button.

Add the stock, maple syrup, and mustard, stirring to scrape up any browned bits. Add the chops and bacon to the pot. Place a steamer basket in the pot over the pork. Put the sweet potatoes in the basket.

Lock the lid in place and turn the valve to Sealing. Press the Pressure Cook button and set the cook time for 10 minutes at high pressure.

When the cooking time is up, let the steam release naturally for 10 minutes, then turn the valve to Venting to quick-release any residual steam. Carefully remove the lid. Transfer the sweet potatoes to a serving bowl, season with salt and pepper, and sprinkle with the pecans. Cover to keep warm. Remove the steamer basket from the pot.

Check the pork for doneness; an instant-read thermometer inserted near (but not touching) the bone should register 140°F (60°C). If not done, cover with a regular pan lid, select Sauté, and adjust to Normal/Medium heat. Simmer, turning, until done, 1–5 minutes longer. Transfer to a platter and tent with foil. In a bowl, stir together the cornstarch and cold water. Add to the pot, select Sauté, and adjust to More/High heat. Simmer, stirring, until the sauce is thickened, 2 minutes. Season to taste. Serve the chops with the sweet potatoes and top with the sauce.

2 tablespoons olive oil

3 slices bacon, coarsely chopped

4 center-cut, bone-in pork chops (each about ½ lb/225 g and 1½ inches/4 cm thick)

Kosher salt and black pepper

1 small yellow onion, chopped

2 tablespoons chopped fresh sage or 2 teaspoons dried sage

2 cloves garlic, chopped

½ cup (120 ml) chicken stock (page 116 or store-bought)

3 tablespoons maple syrup

2 tablespoons whole-grain mustard

2 lb (1 kg) orange-fleshed sweet potatoes, peeled and cut into 2-inch (5-cm) chunks

¼ cup (30 g) toasted chopped pecans

2 tablespoons cornstarch

2 tablespoons cold water

# White Bean & Kale Soup

This hearty, flavorful soup is a staple in northern Italy, where it's ladled over leftover bread. Here the soup is served with little garlic cheese toasts floating on top. Cannellini beans, also called white kidney beans, are available in the bulk section of well-stocked markets and online.

**SERVES 6–8**

In a large bowl, combine the beans, 8 cups (1.9 L) water, and 2 teaspoons salt and soak for at least 12 and up to 24 hours. Drain the beans and rinse with cool water.

Put 1 tablespoon of the oil in the Instant Pot®, select Sauté, and adjust to More/High heat. When the oil is hot, add the bacon and cook, stirring frequently, until crisp and browned, 4–5 minutes. Add the onion, celery, and carrot and cook, stirring frequently, until the vegetables are tender, about 4 minutes. Add the chopped garlic, sage, and rosemary and cook until fragrant, about 45 seconds. Press the Cancel button.

Add the beans, stock, 1 teaspoon salt, ½ teaspoon black pepper, and the red pepper flakes to the pot and stir with a wooden spoon to scrape up any browned bits on the bottom of the pot.

Lock the lid in place and turn the valve to Sealing. Press the Pressure Cook button and set the cook time for 15 minutes at high pressure.

2 cups (400 g) dried cannellini beans, rinsed and picked over

Kosher salt and black pepper

2 tablespoons olive oil

3 slices thick-cut bacon, chopped

1 yellow onion, chopped

2 ribs celery, finely diced

1 large carrot, peeled and finely diced

5 cloves garlic, 4 chopped, 1 left whole

2 tablespoons chopped fresh sage or 2 teaspoons dried sage

2 teaspoons chopped fresh rosemary

4 cups (950 ml) chicken or beef stock (pages 116–117 or store-bought)

Pinch of red pepper flakes

You can substitute white navy or great Northern beans if you must, but keep in mind the texture will be different, as these smaller beans tend to fall apart under high pressure. Serve the soup with a fresh green salad for an easy and nourishing midweek meal.

Meanwhile, preheat the oven to 400°F (200°C). Line a small baking sheet with aluminum foil. Rub the whole garlic clove all over the outside of the baguette; it will feel slightly sticky. Cut the baguette on an angle into ½-inch (12-mm) slices. Lay the slices on the prepared baking sheet, brush with the remaining 1 tablespoon oil, and sprinkle evenly with the cheese. Bake until light golden brown, about 8 minutes. Set the cheese toasts aside.

When the cooking time is up, let the steam release naturally for 15 minutes, then turn the valve to Venting to quick-release any residual steam. Carefully remove the lid and add the kale and marinara sauce. Select Sauté, adjust to Normal/Medium heat, and simmer, stirring occasionally, until the kale is tender, 2–5 minutes. Season to taste with salt and black pepper.

Ladle the soup into bowls, float a few cheese toasts on top of each bowl, and serve.

**TIP** *To make the soup vegetarian, omit the bacon and use vegetable stock instead of chicken stock.*

½ **baguette**

½ **cup (60 g) grated Parmesan cheese**

½ **bunch lacinato kale, thick stems and ribs removed, leaves chopped**

½ **cup (120 ml) marinara sauce**

White Fish Tacos with Mango
Salsa & Lime Crema (page 96)

# SEAFOOD

# Shrimp & Cheesy Grits

In this quick weeknight supper, the cheese grits cook at the same time as the zippy Cajun sauce, thanks to a tall trivet and the "pot-in-pot" method (see page 17). Simmering the shrimp briefly in the sauce right before serving keeps them from overcooking. Cajun seasoning blends vary in spiciness, so taste yours before adding it to the pot to gauge how spicy you'd like this dish to be.

## SERVES 4

To make the Cajun sauce, put the oil in the Instant Pot®, select Sauté, and adjust to More/High heat. When the oil is hot, add the bacon and cook, stirring occasionally, until crisp and browned, 4–5 minutes. Add the onion, bell pepper, celery, and Cajun seasoning and cook, stirring frequently, until the onions are tender, about 4 minutes. Press the Cancel button. Add the tomatoes and stock, stirring with a wooden spoon to scrape up any browned bits.

To make the grits, place a trivet with tall (2-inch/5-cm) feet in the pot over the Cajun mixture. Pour the warm stock into a 7-inch (18-cm) round metal pan with a 6-cup (1.4-L) capacity. Gradually whisk in the grits. Cover tightly with aluminum foil and place on the trivet.

Lock the lid in place and turn the valve to Sealing. Press the Pressure Cook button and set the cook time for 8 minutes at high pressure.

When the cooking time is up, turn the valve to Venting to quick-release the steam. Carefully remove the lid and remove the pan and trivet. Uncover the grits and whisk in the cheese and butter. Season to taste with salt and pepper. Cover and set aside. The grits will thicken as the pan stands.

Select Sauté and adjust to Normal/Medium heat. Add the shrimp to the pot and cook, stirring occasionally, until they are pink and opaque, about 2 minutes. Season the sauce to taste with salt and pepper.

Serve the shrimp and sauce over the grits, with lemon on the side.

### FOR THE CAJUN SAUCE
1 tablespoon olive oil

2 slices bacon, coarsely chopped

1 yellow onion, chopped

1 green or red bell pepper, seeded and chopped

2 ribs celery, chopped

2 teaspoons mild Cajun seasoning blend

½ cup (100 g) chopped tomatoes (fresh or canned)

¼ cup (60 ml) chicken stock (page 116 or store-bought)

### FOR THE GRITS
2⅔ cups (630 ml) chicken stock (page 116) or warm water

¾ cup (120 g) grits or polenta (not quick-cooking)

½ cup (60 g) grated Cheddar cheese

1 tablespoon unsalted butter

Kosher salt and black pepper

1½ lb (680 g) large shrimp, peeled and deveined

1 lemon, quartered

# Dijon Salmon & Vegetable Packets

Cooking fish fillets and thinly cut vegetables together in foil packets in the Instant Pot® seals in the steam and juices without overcooking anything. Serve with steamed rice, orzo, or crusty sourdough bread to mop up the buttery sauce.

## SERVES 4

In a small bowl, using a fork, mash together the butter, mustard, herbs, garlic, and lemon zest until blended. Season with a few pinches of salt.

Have ready 4 pieces of aluminum foil, each 10 inches (25 cm) long. Place a salmon fillet, skin-side down, in the center of each piece of foil. Mound the carrot, bell pepper, and zucchini on the top and sides of the fish, and season with salt and pepper. Spoon big blobs of the butter mixture evenly over the fish and vegetables. Fold up the sides of the foil and seal to form tight packets.

Pour 1 cup (240 ml) water into the pot and place a steam rack/trivet with handles in the pot. Place the packets on the trivet, arranging them in 2 layers.

Lock the lid in place and turn the valve to Sealing. Press the Pressure Cook button and set the cook time for 5 minutes at high pressure.

When the cooking time is up, turn the valve to Venting to quick-release the steam. Carefully remove the lid and transfer the packets to plates. Cut them open at the table (be careful, the escaping steam will be hot!). You can also slide the fish, vegetables, and buttery sauce out of the foil onto plates, if desired.

**TIP** *To prevent overcooking, be sure to use fillets that are about ½ inch (12 mm) thick. These are usually pieces cut from the collar end, as opposed to the thin tail end, of the fish.*

**4 tablespoons (½ stick/ 60 g) unsalted butter, at room temperature**

**4 teaspoons Dijon mustard**

**1 tablespoon mixed minced fresh herbs (dill, flat-leaf parsley, and/or tarragon)**

**1 clove garlic, minced and smashed with side of knife**

**Finely grated zest of ½ lemon**

**Kosher salt**

**4 skin-on salmon or steelhead fillets (5–6 oz/140–170 g each), pin bones removed**

**1 carrot, peeled and julienned**

**1 small red bell pepper, seeded and julienned**

**1 small zucchini, julienned**

**Freshly ground black pepper**

# Lemon Risotto with Crab & Fennel

Craving a luxurious crab dish but don't want to get out the crab crackers and spend a mint to feed the family? This easy recipe is the answer—it's elegant and super quick, and a 1-lb (450-g) container of picked crabmeat feeds four when served alongside creamy, filling risotto.

**SERVES 4**

Put the butter the Instant Pot®, select Sauté, and adjust to More/High heat. When the butter is hot, add the onion, fennel, and carrot and cook, stirring frequently, until the onion is tender, about 5 minutes. Add the rice and cook, stirring frequently, for 1 minute. Add the wine and simmer until nearly evaporated, about 2 minutes. Press the Cancel button.

Add the clam juice and ¾ teaspoon salt, stirring with a wooden spoon to scrape up any browned bits.

Lock the lid in place and turn the valve to Sealing. Press the Pressure Cook button and set the cook time for 8 minutes at high pressure.

Meanwhile, in a bowl, stir together the crabmeat and 1 tablespoon of the dill and half of the lemon zest and juice. Season to taste with salt and black pepper. Set aside at room temperature.

When the cooking time is up, turn the valve to Venting to quick-release the steam. Carefully remove the lid. The risotto will look brothy at first but will thicken as it stands. Add the cayenne and the remaining 1 tablespoon dill and lemon zest and juice. Season to taste with salt and black pepper.

Divide the risotto among 4 bowls. Mound the crabmeat evenly in the center of each bowl and serve.

**TIP** *Look for picked crabmeat in plastic tubs in the seafood department of grocery stores. Drain off any liquid in the container before using.*

**2 tablespoons unsalted butter**

**1 yellow onion, chopped**

**1 small fennel bulb, trimmed, cored, and chopped**

**1 carrot, peeled and finely chopped**

**1 cup (200 g) Arborio rice**

**¼ cup (60 ml) dry white wine**

**2¾ cups (650 ml) clam juice or seafood broth, or chicken stock (page 116 or store-bought)**

**Kosher salt**

**1 lb (450 g) fresh crabmeat, picked over**

**2 tablespoons chopped fresh dill**

**Finely grated zest and juice of ½ lemon**

**Freshly ground black pepper**

**Pinch of cayenne pepper**

*For the best flavor and texture, use solid albacore tuna instead of chunk light tuna, which tends to be mushy.*

# Creamy Tuna Noodle Casserole

Just like the creamy casserole of your childhood but lighter, faster, and tastier! The dried noodles and vegetables cook under pressure first, and then soft whipped cream cheese and solid albacore tuna are stirred into the mixture to make a delicious sauce. The "casserole" is finished with a crisp topping of pan-toasted bread crumbs and Parmesan cheese.

**SERVES 4**

Put 1½ tablespoons of the butter in the Instant Pot®, select Sauté, and adjust to More/High heat. When the butter is hot, add the shallots, celery, mushrooms, and a pinch of salt and cook, stirring frequently, until the vegetables are tender, about 4 minutes. Add the garlic and cook until fragrant, about 30 seconds. Add the wine and simmer until nearly evaporated, about 2 minutes. Press the Cancel button. Stir in the stock. Add the noodles but don't stir.

Lock the lid in place and turn the valve to Sealing. Press the Pressure Cook button and set the cook time for 5 minutes at low pressure.

Meanwhile, in a small nonstick saucepan over medium heat, melt the remaining 1½ tablespoons butter. Add the bread crumbs and cook, stirring occasionally, until golden brown, 3–4 minutes. Sprinkle ¼ cup (30 g) of the Parmesan over the crumbs and cook, stirring constantly, until the cheese is crisp and begins to brown, about 1 minute. Remove from the heat.

Turn the valve to Venting to quick-release the steam. Carefully remove the lid, add the remaining ¼ cup (30 g) Parmesan, the cream cheese, and milk and stir until the cream cheese has melted, about 5 stirs. Fold in the tuna and lemon juice. Season to taste with salt and pepper. Sprinkle with the bread crumbs and serve.

**3 tablespoons unsalted butter**

**2 large shallots, finely chopped**

**2 ribs celery, sliced**

**¼ lb (115 g) shiitake mushrooms, stemmed and brushed clean, caps sliced**

**Kosher salt and black pepper**

**1 clove garlic, chopped**

**¼ cup (60 ml) dry white wine**

**1½ cups (350 ml) vegetable or chicken stock (pages 116–117 or store-bought)**

**½ lb (225 g) dried wide egg noodles**

**1 bread slice, finely ground in a food processor**

**½ cup (60 g) grated Parmesan cheese**

**½ cup (80 g) whipped cream cheese**

**¼ cup (60 ml) whole milk, warmed**

**2 cans (5 oz/142 g each) solid albacore tuna, drained and flaked with a fork**

**1 tablespoon fresh lemon juice**

# Creamy Shrimp Pasta

Jumbo-size frozen shrimp cook perfectly in 5 minutes under low pressure, which also happens to be the perfect timing for dried linguine in a yummy garlic sauce. Don't skip the herbs, as they add a spark of vibrant flavor to this rich dish.

**SERVES 4–6**

Put the oil in the Instant Pot®, select Sauté, and adjust to Normal/ Medium heat. When the oil is hot, add the shallot and cook, stirring frequently, until tender, about 4 minutes. Add the garlic and cook until fragrant, about 30 seconds. Add the wine and simmer until nearly evaporated, about 1 minute. Press the Cancel button.

Add the pasta, fanning it out at different angles to reduce clumping. Add the stock, ½ teaspoon salt, and several grinds of pepper. Place the frozen shrimp on top but don't stir.

Lock the lid in place and turn the valve to Sealing. Press the Pressure Cook button and set the cook time for 5 minutes at low pressure.

When the cooking time is up, turn the valve to Venting to quick-release the steam. Carefully remove the lid and add the cream cheese, tarragon, and lemon zest and juice. Quickly stir with tongs, breaking up any clumps of pasta. Cover with the lid and let stand with the Instant Pot® off for 2–5 minutes to allow the ingredients to finish cooking and absorb some of the liquid. Serve right away.

**TIP** *For the best texture, buy extra-jumbo or jumbo shrimp, also labeled "16/20" and "21/25," respectively. (The numbers indicate how many shrimp are in a pound; the lower the numbers, the larger the shrimp.)*

- 3 tablespoons olive oil
- ¾ cup (90 g) chopped shallot
- 6 cloves garlic, thinly sliced
- ¼ cup (60 ml) dry white wine
- 1 lb (450 g) linguine or spaghetti, broken in half
- 3½ cups (825 ml) chicken stock (page 116 or store-bought)
- Kosher salt and black pepper
- 1 lb (450 g) frozen jumbo or extra-jumbo peeled and deveined shrimp
- ½ cup (80 g) whipped cream cheese
- 2 tablespoons chopped fresh tarragon or dill
- Finely grated zest and juice of ½ lemon

# Bay Scallop & Corn Chowder

For a fresh take on New England clam chowder, this ultra-quick recipe replaces the usual canned clams with tender bay scallops. Corn, dill, and Old Bay seasoning lend additional flavor. The trick here is to cook the vegetables in seafood broth first and then add the delicate scallops and cream just before serving.

**SERVES 4–6**

Put the oil in the Instant Pot®, select Sauté, and adjust to More/High heat. When the oil is hot, add the bacon and cook, stirring occasionally, until crisped, 4–5 minutes. Add the onion and celery and cook, stirring frequently, until tender, about 4 minutes. Add the garlic, 1 teaspoon Old Bay seasoning, and dill and cook until fragrant, about 30 seconds. Press the Cancel button. Add the potatoes, clam juice, and corn, stirring with a wooden spoon to scrape up any browned bits.

Lock the lid in place and turn the valve to Sealing. Press the Pressure Cook button and set the cook time for 3 minutes at high pressure.

When the cooking time is up, turn the valve to Venting to quick-release the steam. Carefully remove the lid.

In a small bowl, stir together the flour and butter until smooth. Add the scallops and cream to the pot. Select Sauté and adjust to Normal/Medium heat. Simmer gently, gradually stirring in the flour-butter mixture, until the scallops are just cooked through and the chowder has thickened, about 4 minutes. Press the Cancel button. Season to taste with salt and pepper and additional Old Bay seasoning, if desired.

Ladle the chowder into bowls and serve.

**TIP** *If your family isn't into scallops, substitute the same quantity of chopped, peeled, and deveined shrimp, firm-fleshed white fish (such as halibut or cod), or salmon.*

1 tablespoon olive oil

1 slice thick-cut bacon, chopped

1 yellow onion, chopped

3 ribs celery, sliced

2 cloves garlic, chopped

1 teaspoon Old Bay seasoning, plus more as needed

1 teaspoon dried dill

1 lb (450 g) red potatoes, cut into ½-inch (12-mm) pieces

1 bottle (8 fl oz/240 ml) clam juice or seafood broth

1 cup (170 g) fresh corn kernels (from 1–2 ears of corn) or frozen corn

1 tablespoon all-purpose flour

1 tablespoon unsalted butter, at room temperature

¾ lb (340 g) bay scallops or diced diver scallops

½ cup (120 ml) heavy cream

Kosher salt and black pepper

# White Fish Tacos with Mango Salsa & Lime Crema

Wahoo is a mild, firm-textured fish that pairs beautifully with a fruity salsa and zesty lime mayo in this Baja-inspired recipe. The frozen fish turns out moist and tender when cooked at high pressure for just 4 minutes, so there's no need to plan ahead. If using fresh fish, reduce the cook time to 2 minutes.

**SERVES 4**

To prepare the lime crema, in a small bowl, stir together the mayonnaise and lime zest and juice; set aside. To prepare the mango salsa, in a medium bowl, stir together the mango, shallot, and cilantro. Season to taste with salt; set aside.

To prepare the fish tacos, pour 1 cup (240 ml) water into the Instant Pot®. Add the reserved lime halves, shallot trimmings, and cilantro stems to impart flavor to the steam. Place a steamer basket in the pot and lightly spray with nonstick cooking spray. Spread the top of the frozen fish fillets with the 1 tablespoon mayonnaise. In a small bowl, stir together the lemon pepper, paprika, cayenne (if using), and ½ teaspoon salt. Sprinkle the seasoning all over the fish and place the fillets on the steamer basket in a single layer.

Lock the lid in place and turn the valve to Sealing. Press the Pressure Cook button and set the cook time for 4 minutes at high pressure.

Meanwhile, wrap the tortillas in damp paper towels and microwave on high until hot, about 2 minutes. Wrap in a cloth napkin or aluminum foil and set aside.

When the cooking time is up, let the steam release naturally for 1 minute, then turn the valve to Venting to quick-release any residual steam. Carefully remove the lid, transfer the fish to a cutting board, and cut into strips. Divide the fish among the tortillas and top with the lime crema, mango salsa, and cabbage. Serve right away.

## FOR THE LIME CREMA AND MANGO SALSA

½ cup (120 ml) mayonnaise

Zest and juice of 1 lime (lime halves reserved)

1 large mango, pitted, peeled, and diced

1 shallot, finely chopped (trimmings reserved)

1 tablespoon chopped fresh cilantro (stems reserved)

Kosher salt

## FOR THE FISH TACOS

1 lb (450 g) frozen wahoo or other firm white fish fillets (at least ¾ inch/2 cm thick)

1 tablespoon mayonnaise

1½ teaspoons lemon pepper

1 teaspoon sweet paprika

Pinch of cayenne pepper (optional)

Kosher salt

8 small (6-inch/15-cm) corn tortillas

2 cups (170 g) finely shredded red cabbage, or coleslaw mix

# Coconut & Ginger Fish Curry

An easy fish curry that tastes like authentic Indian food, this dish is super adaptable—use any seafood that looks good at the market—and it is ready quickly. You can even use frozen fish if you like; just add a few minutes to the cook time.

**SERVES 4**

Put the oil in the Instant Pot®, select Sauté, and adjust to More/High heat. When the oil is hot, add the mustard seeds and curry leaves (if using) and cook until the mustard seeds begin to pop, about 2 minutes. Add the ginger and garlic and cook until fragrant, about 20 seconds. Add the onion and cook, stirring frequently, until beginning to brown, about 5 minutes. Add the tomato, bell pepper, cumin, and turmeric and cook, stirring frequently, until fragrant, about 1 minute. Press the Cancel button.

Add the coconut milk and ½ cup (120 ml) water to the pot, stirring with a wooden spoon to scrape up any browned bits.

Lock the lid in place and turn the valve to Sealing. Press the Pressure Cook button and set the cook time for 5 minutes at high pressure.

When the cooking time is up, turn the valve to Venting to quick-release the steam. Carefully remove the lid and add the fish and garam masala. Select Sauté, adjust to Less/Low heat, and simmer uncovered until the fish is just cooked through, about 5 minutes. Remove the curry leaves and discard. Season to taste with salt and pepper. Sprinkle the curry with the cilantro and serve with the lime wedges on the side.

**TIP** *Curry leaves add a lemony, herbal flavor to curries and soups—they don't taste at all like curry powder. Look for them in well-stocked grocery stores and Indian markets; they're often still attached to their skinny stems. They freeze well, so when you find some, freeze them in a lock-top plastic bag for future Indian meals. They're a real flavor game-changer.*

**2 tablespoons coconut oil or canola oil**

**1 teaspoon brown mustard seeds**

**8 fresh curry leaves (optional) (see Tip)**

**1 tablespoon peeled and minced fresh ginger**

**6 cloves garlic, chopped**

**1 yellow onion, chopped**

**1 large tomato, seeded and chopped**

**1 red or orange bell pepper, seeded and sliced**

**2 teaspoons ground cumin**

**1½ teaspoons ground turmeric**

**1 can (13.5 fl oz/400 ml) coconut milk**

**1½ lb (680 g) skinless firm white fish fillets (such as cod, halibut, or pollack), cut into 1-inch (2.5-cm) pieces**

**1 teaspoon garam masala**

**Kosher salt and black pepper**

**¼ cup (15 g) chopped fresh cilantro**

**1 lime, quartered**

Healthy-ish Macaroni & Cheese
(page 104)

# VEGETARIAN

# Black Bean Chili–Stuffed Sweet Potatoes

These veggie chili–stuffed sweet potatoes are perfect for Meatless Monday—they're easy to make and so filling that no one will miss the meat! Be sure to purchase medium orange-fleshed sweet potatoes that are 10–12 oz (285–340 g) each. Any larger and they won't fit in the pot; any smaller and they'll overcook.

**SERVES 4**

Put the oil in the Instant Pot®, select Sauté, and adjust to More/High heat. When the oil is hot, add the onion, bell pepper, and carrot and cook, stirring frequently, until the onion is tender, about 5 minutes. Add the garlic, chili powder, and cumin and cook until fragrant, about 30 seconds. Add 2 cups (475 ml) water, stirring with a wooden spoon to scrape up any browned bits. Press the Cancel button. Add the black beans and 1 teaspoon salt and stir to combine.

Place a trivet with tall (2-inch/5-cm) feet in the pot over the bean mixture. Place a piece of aluminum foil on the trivet and poke 2 holes in the foil. Prick the sweet potatoes all over with a fork and place them on the foil-lined trivet.

Lock the lid in place and turn the valve to Sealing. Press the Pressure Cook button and set the cook time for 20 minutes at high pressure.

When the cooking time is up, let the steam release naturally for 10 minutes, then turn the valve to Venting to quick-release any residual steam. Carefully remove the lid, transfer the sweet potatoes to a cutting board, and cut in half lengthwise. Season with salt and pepper, cover with foil, and set aside.

Select Sauté, adjust to More/High heat, and simmer uncovered until the chili has thickened and the beans are done, if they are not completely tender, about 5 minutes. Add the lime juice and season the chili to taste with salt and pepper.

Spoon the chili over the sweet potatoes, sprinkle with the cheese, and top with dollops of sour cream and the green onions.

1 tablespoon olive oil

1 yellow onion, chopped

1 red bell pepper, seeded and chopped

1 carrot, peeled and chopped

4 cloves garlic, chopped

2½ tablespoons mild chili powder

1 tablespoon ground cumin

1 cup (200 g) dried black beans, rinsed and picked over

Kosher salt and black pepper

4 medium orange-fleshed sweet potatoes (10–12 oz/285–340 g each)

Juice of ½ lime

1 cup (115 g) grated Cheddar cheese

½ cup (115 g) sour cream

2 green onions, chopped

# Red Beans & Rice

There's no need to pre-soak small red beans for this Cajun-inspired dish; they cook in the same amount of time as the brown rice using the pot-in-pot method (page 17). Look for firm, pre-cooked veggie sausages for this dish. The recipe also works well with fully cooked meat sausages if you'd like to use meat.

**SERVES 4–6**

Put the butter in the Instant Pot®, select Sauté, and adjust to More/High heat. When the butter is hot, add the sausages, onion, bell pepper, and celery and cook, stirring frequently, until the onion is tender, about 5 minutes. Add the garlic and Cajun seasoning and cook until fragrant, about 45 seconds. Press the Cancel button.

Add the red beans, 3 cups (700 ml) water, the bay leaf, and ½ teaspoon salt to the pot. Place a trivet with tall (2-inch/5-cm) feet in the pot over the bean mixture. In a 7-inch (18-cm) round metal pan with a 6-cup (1.4-L) capacity, stir together the rice, 2 cups (475 ml) water, and a generous pinch of salt. Cover tightly with aluminum foil and place on the trivet.

Lock the lid in place and turn the valve to Sealing. Press the Pressure Cook button and set the cook time for 30 minutes at high pressure.

When the cooking time is up, let the steam release naturally for 10 minutes, then turn the valve to Venting to quick-release any residual steam. Carefully remove the lid and remove the pan and trivet. Check the beans to make sure they are tender. (If not, select Sauté, adjust to Normal/Medium heat, place a regular pan lid on the pot, and simmer, stirring occasionally, until the beans are done.)

Season the beans to taste with salt, pepper, and hot sauce. Serve the beans with the rice, sprinkled with the green onions, with additional hot sauce on the side.

**TIP** *Cajun seasoning blends vary in spiciness, so taste yours before adding it to this dish. You can always include more after you feed the kids.*

2 tablespoons unsalted butter

14 oz (400 g) vegetarian andouille or kielbasa sausages, sliced

1 yellow onion, chopped

1 red or green bell pepper, seeded and chopped

3 ribs celery, sliced

4 cloves garlic, chopped

1 tablespoon mild Cajun seasoning blend

1½ cups (300 g) dried small red beans, rinsed and picked over

1 bay leaf

Kosher salt and black pepper

2 cups (400 g) long-grain or short-grain brown rice, rinsed and drained

Hot sauce

3 green onions, chopped

# Noodles with Mixed Veggies & Tofu

Loaded with veggies and protein-rich tofu in a savory Chinese-inspired sauce, these noodles tick all the boxes. Feel free to change things up in this pantry put-together—firm-ish vegetables like sliced carrots, baby corn, bamboo shoots, or water chestnuts will all taste great.

## SERVES 4

Put the canola oil in the Instant Pot®, select Sauté, and adjust to More/High heat. When the oil is hot, add the garlic and ginger and cook until fragrant, about 20 seconds. Press the Cancel button.

Add the carrots, bell pepper, and mushrooms to the pot and stir to combine. Add the stock, hoisin sauce, soy sauce, vinegar, and sesame oil, stirring with a wooden spoon to scrape up any browned bits. Gently stir in the tofu. Fan the pasta over the top of the vegetables and tofu. Gently press down on the noodles to partially submerge them.

Lock the lid in place and turn the valve to Sealing. Press the Pressure Cook button and set the cook time for 5 minutes at high pressure (see Tip).

When the cooking time is up, turn the valve to Venting to quick-release the steam. Carefully remove the lid. Add the cabbage, bean sprouts, and green onions and toss everything together with tongs. Cover with the lid for 1 minute to wilt the vegetables and serve.

**TIP** *Cooking times for linguine vary by brand. To calculate how long yours will take in the Instant Pot®, divide the recommended cooking time on the package by 2 and subtract 1 minute. For instance, if the linguine will take 12 minutes to cook in boiling water, it will require 5 minutes in the Instant Pot®.*

2 tablespoons canola oil

3 cloves garlic, minced

2 teaspoons peeled and minced fresh ginger

2 carrots, peeled and thinly sliced

1 red bell pepper, seeded and thinly sliced

¼ lb (115 g) shiitake mushrooms, stemmed and brushed clean, caps sliced

2 cups (475 ml) vegetable stock (page 117 or store-bought) or water

3 tablespoons hoisin sauce

2 tablespoons low-sodium soy sauce

2 teaspoons rice vinegar

1 teaspoon toasted sesame oil

14 oz (400 g) baked savory or teriyaki-flavored tofu, cut into bite-size cubes

½ lb (225 g) linguine, broken in half

3 cups (250 g) finely shredded green cabbage

1 cup (50 g) bean sprouts

2 green onions, chopped

# Healthy-ish Macaroni & Cheese

Chickpea pasta adds fiber and protein to this one-pot comfort-food classic, while frozen butternut squash melts into the sauce to lend a creamy texture along with fiber and vitamins (and picky eaters will never know it's in there!). Serve with steamed broccoli or a tossed green salad for a complete vegetarian meal.

**SERVES 4**

Put the oil in the Instant Pot®, select Sauté, and adjust to More/High heat. When the oil is hot, add the shallot and cook, stirring frequently, until tender, about 2 minutes. Add the butternut squash and cook, stirring frequently, until falling apart, about 4 minutes. Press the Cancel button.

Using a potato masher, mash the mixture to break up the squash. Add 2 cups (475 ml) water, the pasta, mustard, bay leaf, and 1 teaspoon salt and stir to combine.

Lock the lid in place and turn the valve to Sealing. Press the Pressure Cook button and set the cook time for 3 minutes at high pressure.

When the cooking time is up, turn the valve to Venting to quick-release the steam. Carefully remove the lid and remove the bay leaf and discard. Add the herbed cheese spread and nutmeg and stir until the cheese has melted. Add the Cheddar cheese and stir to combine. Season to taste with salt and pepper and serve right away.

4 teaspoons olive oil

½ cup (70 g) finely chopped shallot or onion

1 package (10 oz/283 g) frozen butternut squash cubes, thawed

½ lb (225 g) chickpea pasta shells or elbows

1½ teaspoons dry mustard

1 bay leaf

Kosher salt and black pepper

¼ cup (60 g) plus 2 tablespoons soft herbed cheese spread (such as Boursin or Laughing Cow)

¼ teaspoon ground nutmeg

½ cup (60 g) grated Cheddar cheese

Chopped fresh flat-leaf parsley or basil leaves make a vibrant, aromatic garnish for this hearty and nourishing dish.

# Black Bean & Cheese Tamales

Folding masa dough around the cheesy black-bean filling and wrapping it in corn husks takes a little time, but it's a fun project for adults and kids alike. The Instant Pot® cuts the tamale steaming time in half.

**SERVES 6–8**

To make the tamales, separate the corn husks, discarding any corn silk stuck between the layers. Put the corn husks in a large pot, cover with hot water, and place a plate on top to keep them submerged. Soak until pliable, about 1 hour.

Meanwhile, make the dough: In a large bowl, whisk together the masa, baking powder, and 1 teaspoon salt. Add the stock and stir until absorbed. Add the coconut oil and stir until the dough comes together. It will be sticky at first but will firm up as the coconut oil cools and the masa absorbs the stock. You want a smooth, pliable dough. After 10 minutes, if the dough is too sticky to handle, add more masa, 1 tablespoon at a time, until a smooth, moist dough forms. Cover and set aside.

To make the filling, in a medium bowl, combine the black beans, green chiles, taco seasoning, and cheese. Using a fork, mash about one-fourth of the beans so the filling will be sticky and stay inside the tamales. Set aside.

Drain the corn husks and pat dry. Place a husk on a work surface with the narrow end facing you. Place about 3 tablespoons of the dough on the top third (the widest part) of the husk and pat down with moistened fingers to form a thin layer of dough in a rough 4-by-5-inch (10-by-13-cm) rectangle. Spread a vertical stripe of the black bean filling (about a heaping tablespoon) down the center of the masa rectangle.

## FOR THE TAMALES

**20 large corn husks**

**4 cups (480 g) corn masa mix (masa harina), plus more as needed**

**1½ teaspoons baking powder**

**Kosher salt**

**3 cups (700 ml) vegetable stock (page 117 or store-bought) or water**

**⅔ cup (140 g) coconut oil, melted**

This recipe yields about 16 tamales, but it's helpful to have some extra husks on hand in case a few are too small to use for wrapping. Plan on 2–3 tamales per person for a meal-size portion.

Fold the left side of the husk up and over the filling. Peel back the husk so the dough releases from the husk and covers the left half of the filling. Fold the right side of the husk over the filling in the same way, so the dough from the right side of the tamale meets the left side of the dough in the middle. Fold the left and right sides of the husk back over the tamale to encase it. Fold up the narrow bottom end of the husk over the filled part of the tamale. Tie with kitchen twine. Repeat with the remaining husks, dough, and filling.

Pour 1 cup (240 ml) water into the Instant Pot® and place a steaming basket in the pot. Arrange the tamales upright on the basket, open end up.

Lock the lid in place and turn the valve to Sealing. Press the Pressure Cook button and set the cook time for 40 minutes at high pressure.

When the cooking time is up, let the steam release naturally for 10 minutes, then turn the valve to Venting to quick-release any residual steam. Carefully remove the lid and transfer the tamales to a plate. Let stand for 10 minutes to firm up. Serve with taco sauce.

**TIP** *Steamed tamales freeze well. Organize a tamale wrapping party and double the recipe, then cook them in two batches. Store cooled, cooked tamales in lock-top plastic bags in the freezer for up to 6 months. To reheat, wrap individual frozen tamales in damp paper towels and microwave until heated through, 2–3 minutes.*

FOR THE FILLING

1 can (15 oz/425 g) black beans, rinsed and drained, or 1½ cups (250 g) home-cooked black beans (page 121)

1 can (4 oz/113 g) mild diced green chiles, drained

1 tablespoon taco seasoning

½ cup (60 g) grated Cheddar or Monterey jack cheese

2 cups (475 ml) taco sauce or salsa

# Broccoli & Everything Bagel Strata

This lovely bread-and-egg casserole, which features savory "everything" bagels, Cheddar, and broccoli, is equally at home on the breakfast and the dinner table. It's vegetarian, but feel free to add a bit of cooked Italian sausage, diced ham, or crumbled bacon if you'd like.

**SERVES 4–6**

Spray a 7-inch (18-cm) round metal pan with a 6-cup (1.4-L) capacity thoroughly with nonstick cooking spray. Spray a 12-inch (30-cm) length of aluminum foil with cooking spray.

In a large bowl, toss together the bagels, broccoli, and green onions and transfer to the prepared baking dish. In a medium bowl, whisk together the eggs, half-and-half, lemon zest, nutmeg, ¾ teaspoon salt, and a few grinds of pepper. Gradually pour the egg mixture over the bagel mixture, pressing down with a spatula so the bagels will absorb the eggs. Sprinkle with the cheese. Cover the dish tightly with the prepared foil, sprayed-side down.

Pour 2 cups (475 ml) water into the Instant Pot®. Place a trivet with tall (2-inch/5-cm) feet in the pot and place the dish on the trivet.

Lock the lid in place and turn the valve to Sealing. Press the Pressure Cook button and set the cook time for 15 minutes at high pressure.

When the cooking time is up, let the steam release naturally for 15 minutes, then turn the valve to Venting to quick-release any residual steam. Carefully remove the lid.

Blot the top of the foil with a paper towel to absorb excess moisture. Using tongs, transfer the dish to a heatproof surface. Remove the foil, cut the strata into wedges, and serve.

3 "everything" bagels (¾ lb/ 340 g), cut into ¼-inch (6-mm) pieces

8 oz (225 g) broccoli crowns, finely chopped

2 green onions, chopped

6 large eggs

1¼ cups (300 ml) half-and-half or whole milk

1½ teaspoons finely grated lemon zest

½ teaspoon ground nutmeg

Kosher salt and black pepper

½ cup (60 g) grated Cheddar cheese

# Creamy Tomato Soup & Cheese Tortellini

A bowl of steamy tomato soup is the ultimate comfort food. Add tortellini and a touch of cream and you've taken it over the top. Use high-quality dried tortellini (such as Barilla or DaVinci); fresh refrigerated tortellini will fall apart under the high pressure of the Instant Pot®.

### SERVES 4

Put the oil in the Instant Pot®, select Sauté, and adjust to More/High heat. When the oil is hot, add the onion and carrot and cook, stirring frequently, until the onions are tender, about 4 minutes. Add the garlic and basil and cook until fragrant, about 45 seconds. Press the Cancel button.

Add the stock, tomatoes, brown sugar, bay leaf, and ½ teaspoon each salt and pepper to the pot, stirring with a wooden spoon to scrape up any browned bits. Stir in the tortellini.

Lock the lid in place and turn the valve to Sealing. Press the Pressure Cook button and set the cook time for 10 minutes at high pressure.

When the cooking time is up, let the steam release naturally for 10 minutes, then turn the valve to Venting to quick-release any residual steam. Carefully remove the lid and remove the bay leaf and discard. Stir in the cream and season to taste with salt and pepper.

Ladle the soup into bowls and serve.

**TIP** *To make this a pasta-and-sauce dish instead of soup, omit the carrot, reduce the stock to 3 cups (700 ml), and substitute a thin marinara sauce for the crushed tomatoes. Serve with a sprinkle of grated Parmesan cheese.*

**2 tablespoons olive oil**

**1 yellow onion, chopped**

**1 large carrot, peeled and chopped**

**3 cloves garlic, chopped**

**1 teaspoon dried basil**

**4 cups (950 ml) vegetable or chicken stock (pages 116–117 or store-bought)**

**2 cups (500 g) canned crushed tomatoes with basil**

**1 tablespoon firmly packed light brown sugar**

**1 bay leaf**

**Kosher salt and black pepper**

**½ lb (225 g) dried cheese or spinach tortellini**

**½ cup (120 ml) heavy cream**

# Corn & Zucchini Chowder

Corncobs impart incredible corn flavor to this delicious golden soup, so it's worth shaving the fresh kernels off the cob. The cream adds extra richness but can be omitted if you'd prefer a vegan soup. You can also substitute a different summer squash for the zucchini.

**SERVES 4–6**

To cut the kernels off the cob, hold an ear of corn upright on a cutting board. Using a sharp chef's knife, cut down the length of the cob to remove the kernels. Repeat with the remaining ears of corn. Set the kernels and corncobs aside.

Put the oil in the Instant Pot®, select Sauté, and adjust to More/High heat. When the oil is hot, add the onion and cook, stirring frequently, until tender, about 4 minutes. Add the garlic and 2 teaspoons Old Bay seasoning and cook until fragrant, about 30 seconds. Press the Cancel button.

Add 4 ½ cups (1.1 L) water, the corncobs, potatoes, and bay leaves to the pot, stirring with a wooden spoon to scrape up any browned bits.

Lock the lid in place and turn the valve to Sealing. Press the Pressure Cook button and set the cook time for 7 minutes at high pressure.

When the cooking time is up, turn the valve to Venting to quick-release the steam. Carefully remove the lid. Remove the corncobs and bay leaves and discard. Stir in the corn kernels, zucchini, and cream. Select Sauté, adjust to Normal/Medium heat, and simmer, stirring occasionally, until the corn and zucchini are just tender, about 5 minutes. Season to taste with salt and pepper and more Old Bay seasoning, if you like.

Ladle the chowder into bowls and serve.

**6 ears of corn, shucked**

**2 tablespoons olive oil**

**1 yellow onion, chopped**

**3 cloves garlic, minced**

**2 teaspoons Old Bay seasoning, plus more as needed**

**4 red potatoes, cut into ¾-inch (2-cm) pieces**

**2 bay leaves**

**2 zucchini, halved lengthwise and cut into half-moons ¼ inch (6 mm) thick**

**1 cup (240 ml) heavy cream**

**Kosher salt and black pepper**

# Veggie Fried Rice with Cashews

This time-saving one-pot recipe cooks the rice and veggies at the same time using the "pot-in-pot" method (page 17). When they're tossed together with the raw eggs after the pressure is released, the heat from the rice cooks the eggs perfectly. The recipe is a blank canvas—add sliced mushrooms, diced ham, or tofu to the pot, or swap in shelled edamame or sliced snow peas for the frozen peas.

### SERVES 4

Put the oil in the Instant Pot®, select Sauté, and adjust to Normal/Medium heat. When the oil is hot, add the carrots, celery, and water chestnuts and cook, stirring frequently, until the vegetables are beginning to brown, about 4 minutes. Add the garlic and ginger and cook until fragrant, 30 seconds. Press the Cancel button.

Add the stock, the 2 tablespoons soy sauce, and vinegar to the pot, stirring with a wooden spoon to scrape up any browned bits. Place a trivet with tall (2-inch/5-cm) feet in the pot over the vegetable mixture. In a 7-inch (18-cm) round metal pan with a 6-cup (1.4-L) capacity, stir together the rice and 1½ cups (355 ml) water. Place the uncovered pan on the trivet.

Lock the lid in place and turn the valve to Sealing. Press the Pressure Cook button and set the cook time for 5 minutes at high pressure.

When the cooking time is up, turn the valve to Venting to quick-release the steam. Carefully remove the lid and remove the pan and trivet. Pour the rice into the pot with the vegetables. Add the eggs, peas, cashews, and green onions and stir well so the eggs coat the rice. Cover with the lid and let stand with the Instant Pot® off for 1 minute to gently cook the eggs.

Season the fried rice to taste with soy sauce and pepper and serve right away.

3 tablespoons toasted sesame oil

2 large carrots, peeled and diced

2 ribs celery, sliced

1 can (8 oz/227 g) sliced water chestnuts, drained

3 cloves garlic, chopped

1 tablespoon peeled and chopped fresh ginger

½ cup (120 ml) vegetable or chicken stock (pages 116–117 or store-bought)

2 tablespoons low-sodium soy sauce, plus more as needed

1 tablespoon rice vinegar

1½ cups (300 g) long-grain white rice, rinsed and drained

2 large eggs, lightly beaten

½ cup (70 g) frozen peas or edamame, thawed

½ cup (70 g) roasted cashews

3 green onions, sliced

Freshly ground black pepper

# Thai Butternut Squash & Tofu Soup with Peanut-Cilantro Relish

Thai curry paste and coconut milk marry beautifully with sweet butternut squash in this satisfying soup. Lime leaves are available in the produce section of some grocery stores or at Asian markets. Although optional here, they are worth seeking out, as they add a mouthwatering lime-and-floral flavor that makes the dish taste authentically Thai. Leftover lime leaves freeze well.

**SERVES 4**

To make the soup, put the oil in the Instant Pot®, select Sauté, and adjust to More/High heat. Add the onion and bell pepper and cook, stirring frequently, until the vegetables are tender, about 5 minutes. Add the curry paste and cook, stirring constantly, until fragrant, about 15 seconds. Press the Cancel button.

Add the butternut squash, coconut milk, stock, and lime leaves (if using) to the pot and stir to combine.

Lock the lid in place and turn the valve to Sealing. Press the Pressure Cook button and set the cook time for 4 minutes at high pressure.

Meanwhile, make the relish: Mound the cilantro, peanuts, garlic, and lime zest on a cutting board. Chop until the cilantro and peanuts are broken down into confetti-size bits.

When the cooking time is up, turn the valve to Venting to quick-release the steam. Carefully remove the lid and remove the lime leaves and discard. Stir in the tofu and season to taste with soy sauce. Let stand for a few minutes to heat up the tofu.

Ladle the soup into bowls, top with the peanut-cilantro relish, and serve.

**TIP** *If you're serving vegetarians, be sure to check the curry paste label; some brands contain dried shrimp or fish sauce.*

## FOR THE SOUP

**2 tablespoons coconut oil or canola oil**

**1 yellow onion, chopped**

**1 red bell pepper, seeded and sliced**

**2 tablespoons vegetarian red curry paste (see Tip)**

**2 lb (1 kg) butternut squash, peeled, seeded, and cut into 1-inch (2.5-cm) cubes**

**1 can (13.5 fl oz/400 ml) coconut milk**

**3 cups (700 ml) vegetable stock (page 117 or store-bought)**

**6 Thai lime leaves (optional)**

## FOR THE RELISH

**½ cup (15 g) loosely packed fresh cilantro leaves**

**¼ cup (35 g) dry-roasted peanuts**

**1 small clove garlic, peeled**

**Zest of 1 lime**

**14 oz (400 g) firm tofu, cut into ½-inch (12-mm) cubes**

**Soy sauce or fish sauce**

# Risotto with Miso & Shiitake "Bacon"

This savory Asian spin on risotto gets its umami from miso soup—either boxed miso broth or instant miso soup mix, available where Asian ingredients are sold and in the soup section of most grocery stores. The baked shiitake mushroom "bacon" topping adds the perfect counterpoint to the creamy rice. Garnish with nori flakes or vegetarian furikake, if you like.

**SERVES 4**

To make the shiitake "bacon," preheat the oven to 375°F (190°C). Line a baking sheet with parchment paper or aluminum foil and spray with nonstick cooking spray. In a bowl, toss together the mushrooms, oil, maple syrup, garlic powder, paprika, and ⅛ teaspoon pepper. Transfer to the prepared baking sheet and spread in a single layer. Bake, stirring occasionally, until browned and crisp, 20–30 minutes. Set aside.

Meanwhile, make the risotto: Put the butter in the Instant Pot®, select Sauté, and adjust to More/High heat. When the butter is hot, add the onion and cook, stirring frequently, until tender, about 4 minutes. Add the rice and cook, stirring frequently, for 1 minute. Add the sake and simmer for 1 minute until nearly evaporated. Press the Cancel button.

Add the miso soup broth, stirring with a wooden spoon to scrape up any browned bits.

Lock the lid in place and turn the valve to Sealing. Press the Pressure Cook button and set the cook time for 8 minutes at high pressure.

When the cooking time is up, turn the valve to Venting to quick-release the steam. Carefully remove the lid. Add the spinach and lemon juice and stir until the spinach is wilted. Season the risotto to taste with salt and pepper and let stand uncovered for 2 minutes. (The rice will absorb more liquid as it stands.)

Divide the risotto among 4 bowls, sprinkle with the shiitake "bacon," and serve.

### FOR THE SHIITAKE "BACON"
½ **lb (225 g) shiitake mushrooms, stemmed and brushed clean, caps thinly sliced**

4 **teaspoons toasted sesame oil**

1 **tablespoon maple syrup**

½ **teaspoon garlic powder**

¼ **teaspoon smoked paprika**

**Freshly ground black pepper**

### FOR THE RISOTTO
2 **tablespoons unsalted butter**

1 **cup (115 g) chopped sweet onion**

1 **cup (200 g) Arborio rice**

½ **cup (120 ml) dry sake or white wine**

3 **cups (700 ml) vegetarian miso soup broth or prepared miso soup mix**

2 **cups (60 g) loosely packed baby spinach leaves**

1 **tablespoon fresh lemon juice**

**Kosher salt and black pepper**

# Homemade Stock

We can probably all agree that any dish made with homemade stock tastes better than those made with the store-bought version. While meat stocks used to require the better part of an afternoon to prepare, with this method you can shave hours off that time and eliminate the need to keep an eye on the stockpot. Store extra in the freezer to have on hand for quick weeknight meals.

**MAKES ABOUT 3 QT (3 L)**

## CHICKEN STOCK

Season the chicken with the salt. Select Sauté on the the Instant Pot® and heat the oil. Working in batches, brown the chicken on both sides, about 3 minutes per side. Transfer to a plate as browned. Add the onion and carrots to the pot and cook, stirring occasionally, until browned, about 2 minutes. Add 1 cup (250 ml) water and bring to a simmer, stirring occasionally with a wooden spoon to scrape up any browned bits. Press the Cancel button.

Return the chicken to the pot and add the garlic, parsley, thyme, bay leaves, peppercorns, and 11 cups (2.75 L) water, ensuring that the pot is no more than two-thirds full. Lock the lid in place and turn the valve to Sealing. Press the Pressure Cook button and set the cook time for 1 hour at high pressure.

Let the steam release naturally. Carefully remove the lid. Pour the stock through a fine-mesh sieve into a large bowl. Discard the solids. If desired, pour the broth into a fat separator to remove the fat (or chill the broth in the refrigerator until the fat solidifies on top, then remove it with a spoon). Let the stock cool completely, then ladle into airtight storage containers. Refrigerate for up to 4 days or freeze for up to 3 months.

**3 lb (1.5 kg) chicken parts (drumsticks, backs, necks, and wings)**

**2 teaspoons kosher salt**

**1 tablespoon olive oil**

**1 yellow onion, quartered**

**2 carrots, cut into 3-inch (7.5-cm) pieces**

**2 cloves garlic, smashed**

**3 fresh flat-leaf parsley sprigs**

**3 fresh thyme sprigs**

**2 bay leaves**

**¼ teaspoon whole black peppercorns**

**TIP** *You can skip the browning step and put all of the raw ingredients into the pot instead, but keep in mind that the flavor will be milder.*

**MAKES ABOUT 2½ QT (2.5 L)**

# VEGETABLE STOCK

Combine all the ingredients in the Instant Pot® and add 10 cups (2.5 L) water, ensuring that the pot is no more than two-thirds full. Lock the lid in place and turn the valve to Sealing. Press the Pressure Cook button and set the cook time for 30 minutes at high pressure.

Let the steam release naturally. Carefully remove the lid. Pour the stock through a fine-mesh sieve into a large bowl. Discard the solids. Let the stock cool completely, then ladle into airtight storage containers. Refrigerate for up to 4 days or freeze for up to 3 months.

**2 yellow onions, roughly chopped**

**2 ribs celery, roughly chopped**

**2 carrots, roughly chopped**

**1 cup (90 g) white button or cremini mushrooms, brushed clean and roughly sliced**

**4 cloves garlic, smashed**

**4 fresh flat-leaf parsley sprigs**

**2 bay leaves**

**1 teaspoon whole black peppercorns**

**MAKES ABOUT 2 QT (2 L)**

# BEEF STOCK

Combine all the ingredients in the Instant Pot® and add 8 cups (2 L) water, ensuring that the pot is no more than two-thirds full. Lock the lid in place and turn the valve to Sealing. Press the Pressure Cook button and set the cook time for 2 hours at high pressure.

Let the steam release naturally. Carefully remove the lid. Pour the stock through a fine-mesh sieve into a large bowl. Discard the solids. If desired, pour the broth into a fat separator to remove the fat (or chill the broth in the refrigerator until the fat solidifies on top, then remove it with a spoon). Let the stock cool completely, then ladle into airtight storage containers. Refrigerate for up to 4 days or freeze for up to 3 months.

**3 lb (1.5 kg) beef marrowbones, cracked by a butcher**

**2 thick slices (about 1 lb/450 g) meaty beef shin**

**2 carrots, roughly chopped**

**2 ribs celery, roughly chopped**

**1 large yellow onion, roughly chopped**

**4 fresh flat-leaf parsley sprigs**

**1 bay leaf**

**8–10 whole black peppercorns**

## VARIATION

**Bone Broth:** *Roast the beef marrowbones for 30–40 minutes in a preheated 450°F (230°C) oven. Add 1–2 tablespoons apple cider vinegar to the pot with the other ingredients and cook at high pressure for 3 hours.*

*Release the steam naturally. (The bone broth has cooked long enough if the bones crumble when touched and the tendons, cartilage, and connective tissue have dissolved.) Strain and store the broth as directed above.*

# Quick Steamed Veggies

Instant Pot® steaming is a great choice for cooking vegetables, particularly hearty root vegetables, which are ready in half the amount of time required for other cooking methods. A quick, creamy dressing makes the ideal accompaniment.

## VEGGIES

Pour 1 cup (240 ml) water into the Instant Pot®. Place the vegetables in a steamer basket or ovenproof bowl and set it on a steam rack with handles. Using the handles, lower the steamer basket and steam rack into the pot. Lock the lid in place and turn the valve to Sealing. Press the Pressure Cook button and set the cook time for 4–6 minutes (about 2 minutes per pound/500 g) at high pressure.

Meanwhile, make the dressing. Combine the avocado, yogurt, oil, ⅓ cup (75 ml) water, herbs, and lemon juice in a food processor or blender and process until smooth. Add salt and pepper to taste. Transfer to a small pitcher or jar.

When the vegetables have finished cooking, turn the valve to Venting to quick-release the steam. When the steam stops, carefully remove the lid and, using the steam rack handles, lift out the steamer basket.

Transfer the vegetables to a large bowl and serve with dressing alongside.

**2–3 lb (1–1.4 kg) vegetables, such as broccoli florets, cauliflower florets, broccolini, carrots, parsnips, squash, sugar snap peas, haricots verts, and/or asparagus, cut into similar-size pieces**

FOR THE DRESSING

**1 avocado, halved, pitted, and scooped from skin**

**¼ cup (65 g) plain or Greek yogurt**

**2 tablespoons avocado oil**

**½ cup (10 g) loosely packed fresh dill, parsley, or cilantro sprigs, or a combo**

**¼ cup (60 ml) fresh lemon juice**

**Kosher salt and black pepper**

# Quick Steamed Potatoes

This foolproof method will work with any variety of potato—just be sure to cut the potatoes into 2-inch (5-cm) pieces. Try red new potatoes in potato salad (see recipe below) for a low-fat addition to a casual party, family barbecue, or picnic.

## POTATOES

Pour 2 cups (475 ml) water into the Instant Pot® and insert a steam rack. Put the potatoes in a steamer basket and set it on the rack. Lock the lid in place and turn the valve to Sealing. Press the Pressure Cook button and set the cook time for 8 minutes at high pressure.

When the cooking time is up, turn the valve to Venting to quick-release the steam. When the steam stops, carefully remove the lid. Transfer the potatoes to a serving bowl. Toss with a few pats of butter (if using), season with salt and pepper, and serve, or use as desired.

**3 lb (1.5 kg) potatoes, such as russet or Yukon gold, cut into 2-inch (5-cm) cubes**

**Unsalted butter (optional)**

**Kosher salt and black pepper**

### VARIATION

**Quick Potato Salad:** *In a medium bowl, stir together ⅓ cup (35 g) thinly sliced red onion and 3 tablespoons red wine vinegar. Let stand until the onion softens slightly, about 5 minutes. In a small bowl, whisk together 1 tablespoon red wine vinegar, ¼ cup (60 ml) olive oil, and 2 tablespoons Dijon mustard. Stir into the onion mixture and season with salt and pepper. Set the vinaigrette aside.*

*In a large bowl, combine 3 lb (1.5 kg) quick-steamed Yukon gold, fingerling, or new potatoes (see recipe above), 6 thinly sliced radishes, and the vinaigrette and toss to combine. Season with salt and pepper. Top the potato salad with 2 peeled and sliced large hard-boiled eggs (optional) and 2 tablespoons coarsely chopped fresh dill. Serve warm or at room temperature, or refrigerate up to overnight and serve chilled.*

# Rice

Cooking rice can be a daunting task, not to mention a long one, when it comes to brown and wild rice varieties. This method is speedy and can be easily adjusted for your texture preference. If you like softer rice, add ¼ cup (60 ml) more water to the pot at the beginning, or let the steam release naturally for a longer period of time.

**MAKES ABOUT 4 CUPS (640 G)**

## WHITE RICE

Combine the rice, salt, and 2 cups (475 ml) water in the Instant Pot®. Lock the lid in place and turn the valve to Sealing. Press the Pressure Cook button and set the cook time for 4 minutes at high pressure.

Let the steam release naturally for 10 minutes, then turn the valve to Venting to quick-release any residual steam. Carefully remove the lid and fluff the rice with a fork. If the rice feels too moist, place a dish towel over the pot and let the moisture evaporate for a few minutes longer, until your desired texture is reached.

**2 cups (400 g) long-grain white rice, such as jasmine or basmati**

**½ teaspoon kosher salt**

**MAKES ABOUT 4 CUPS (800 G)**

## BROWN RICE

Combine the rice, salt, and 2½ cups (600 ml) water in the Instant Pot®. Lock the lid in place and turn the valve to Sealing. Press the Pressure Cook button and set the cook time for 15 minutes at high pressure.

Let the steam release naturally for 10 minutes, then turn the valve to Venting to quick-release any residual steam. Carefully remove the lid and fluff the rice with a fork. If the rice feels too moist, place a dish towel over the pot and let the moisture evaporate for a few minutes longer, until your desired texture is reached.

**2 cups (370 g) long-grain brown rice**

**½ teaspoon kosher salt**

# Beans

Although canned beans are very convenient, they just don't taste the same as the home-cooked kind. The absolute best part about preparing beans in the Instant Pot® is that they don't need to be soaked ahead of time. For bigger batches, double the quantities of beans, water, and oil.

**MAKES ABOUT 3 CUPS (540 G)**

## BASIC BEANS

Combine the beans, 4 cups (1 L) water, oil, and salt to taste in the Instant Pot®. Lock the lid in place and turn the valve to Sealing. Press the Beans/Chili button and set the cook time for the cooking time designated in the chart below at high pressure.

Let the steam release naturally, or for at least 15 minutes, before turning the valve to Venting to quick-release any residual steam. When the steam stops, carefully remove the lid. Drain the beans in a colander set in the sink.

**TIP** *If you would prefer to soak your beans, soak 1 cup (200 g) of beans in 4 cups (1 L) water for at least 4 hours or up to 12 hours, then cook them in their soaking water. They will cook in about half the time needed for unsoaked beans.*

1 cup (200 g) dried beans, chickpeas, or lentils, rinsed and picked over

1 teaspoon canola oil

1–2 teaspoons kosher salt

**COOKING TIMES FOR UNSOAKED BEANS & LENTILS**

| | |
|---|---|
| Green, Brown, or Black Lentils | 15 minutes |
| Black Beans | 20–25 minutes |
| Navy Beans | 20–25 minutes |
| Pinto Beans | 20–25 minutes |
| Cannellini Beans | 35–40 minutes |
| Chickpeas | 35–40 minutes |

# Grains

Polenta and quinoa cook quickly in the Instant Pot® and are terrific nutrient-rich bases for bowls or other easy meals. Once the polenta has been stirred into the pot, you can set it and forget it—avoiding the nearly constant stirring required of traditional stove-top polenta.

**MAKES 2½ CUPS (625 G)**

## POLENTA

Select Sauté on the Instant Pot®. Add the liquid and 2 teaspoons salt and bring to a boil. Slowly stream in the polenta, whisking constantly to prevent clumping.

Press the Cancel button. Lock the lid in place and turn the valve to Sealing. Press the Pressure Cook button and set the cook time for 8 minutes at high pressure.

Turn the valve to Venting to quick-release the steam. When the steam stops, carefully remove the lid.

Season the polenta to taste with salt and pepper. Stir in the butter and cheese (if using) and serve.

**4 cups (1 L) liquid, such as water, whole milk, and/or chicken stock (page 116 or store-bought)**

**Kosher salt and black pepper**

**1 cup (160 g) polenta**

**2 tablespoons unsalted butter (optional)**

**½ cup (60 g) freshly grated Parmesan cheese (optional)**

**MAKES ABOUT 3 CUPS (330 G)**

## QUINOA

Put the quinoa, 1¼ cups (300 ml) water, and salt in the Instant Pot®. Stir to combine.

Lock the lid in place and turn the valve to Sealing. Press the Pressure Cook button and set the cook time for 1 minute at high pressure.

Let the steam release naturally for 10 minutes, then turn the valve to Venting to quick-release any residual steam. Carefully remove the lid and fluff the quinoa with a fork.

**1 cup (180 g) quinoa (red, white, or mixed), rinsed**

**½ teaspoon kosher salt**

Chicken Adobo Quinoa Burrito Bowls (page 36)

# INDEX

White Fish Tacos with Mango
Salsa & Lime Crema (page 96)

# INSTANT POT® FAMILY MEALS

Conceived and produced by Weldon Owen International
in collaboration with Williams Sonoma, Inc.
3250 Van Ness Avenue, San Francisco, CA 94109

## A WELDON OWEN PRODUCTION

1150 Brickyard Cove Road
Richmond, CA 94801
www.weldonowen.com

Printed in China
10 9 8 7 6 5 4 3 2 1

Library of Congress
Cataloging-in-Publication data is available.

ISBN: 978-1-68188-502-5

## WELDON OWEN INTERNATIONAL

CEO Raoul Goff
President Kate Jerome
Publisher Roger Shaw
Associate Publisher Amy Marr
Senior Editor Lisa Atwood
Creative Director Chrissy Kwasnik
Designer Megan Sinead Harris

Managing Editor Tarji Rodriguez
Production Manager Binh Au
Imaging Manager Don Hill

Photographer Erin Scott
Food Stylist Lillian Kang
Prop Stylist Claire Mack

## ACKNOWLEDGMENTS

Weldon Owen wishes to thank the following people
for their generous support in producing this book:
Kris Balloun, Josephine Hsu, Bronwyn Lane, Veronica Laramie,
Ivy Manning, Rachel Markowitz, Alexis Mersel,
Nicola Parisi, Elizabeth Parson, and Jourdan Plautz.